On Drawing Rocks

Written and Illustrated by
Marjory Kron
Layout by Helane Freeman

Marjory Kron
Vilimapubco
Malibu, CA
marjorykron@gmail.com

For permission requests, sales to U.S. bookstores and wholesalers, or to inquire about quantity discounts, please contact the publisher at the email address above.

Printed in the United States of America

Library of Congress Control Number: 2017913462

ISBN 978-0-9988792-7-7

First Edition
10 9 8 7 6 5 4 3 2 1

On Drawing Rocks

Marjory Kron

Acknowledgements

There isn't a person in my life who hasn't influenced me in some way
and become a part of my foundation.

Some are mentioned in this book, and some are not, but I thank
every one for the lessons each experience has taught me,
and I assure you that you are always carried with me.

Marjory Kron-Rucker

Preface

By the year 2016 Marjory had completed two art books, _In My Mind's Eye_ and _Observations_. She was working on her third book unfortunately interrupted by her untimely death. For a while it was affectionately called _The Rock Book,_ but it has finally been named _On Drawing Rocks_.

Part 1 shows photographic stills taken from an educational video made by her son-in-law, Thomas Rincker.

Part 2 shows the bulk of her brilliant Prismacolor pencil artwork.

Part 3 shows Marge actively collecting material for her drawings.

Part 4 shows Marge's irrepressible energy, her unique capacity for love, and her endearing sense of humor.

Table of Content

A talk about drawing rocks

Doing a drawing like this is an adventure - full of mysteries, the unexpected, disappearances and discoveries. People say to me, "How do you have the patience for it? It looks like it takes forever!" And I reply, "Every minute is a revelation." The picture and I are in a conversation. I put down a stroke and the picture tells me what it needs next. I put down another stroke and the picture answers again. Each mark I make tells me something about what to do next. I am in constant communication with what is happening on the page. Many artists work this way. That's the fun! The time it takes is not important. Patience is not an issue if the artist is fully engaged. The process is the thing.

In this process each stroke has it's purpose and is put down mindfully one stroke depending on the next to build the form. Within any small area all kinds of connections may be occurring. How does one color play against another color? How much texture or detail is needed? Should one area be left smooth to contrast with another? What do the shadows and highlights tell us about the shape of the rocks and their relationship to one another?

As the drawing progresses interesting things happen spontaneously on the page. These can be developed and used as part of the picture. This is one of the most engaging parts of the process. It keeps me on my toes to draw deliberately, carefully, watchfully, paying close attention to what is emerging on the paper, ready to use any "accident" that works.

Of course, patience can be a struggle at times, especially when things are not coming out the way I think they should. Changes or corrections have to be made and an anxious irritation can take hold. What to do? How to fix it? Is the whole picture lost? At such times I just walk away - let my subconscious mind take care of it while I do something else. When I come back and take a fresh look, I usually see my mistake and can imagine other possibilities. At this point I need to do some careful demolition, which means erasing and drawing over what I had previously done. There is great creative potential at such times when underlying layers of drawing are revealed. I erase watchfully, noticing what emerges as I go. Some of the richest and most beautiful areas of a drawing may come out of the process of correction. Ultimately, drawing one section involves being aware of how that section fits in relation to all the other sections - size, color, method of application, sources of light must all work-together to finally create a unified, consistent larger picture.

But where is the starting point, you might ask? How do you begin? For me the answer is in the core idea, which inspires, informs and unifies the piece. In these drawings I have been inspired by the rocks themselves - the stories that their amazing erosions reveal, their sensual surfaces, their subtle colors, the lacy patterns carved into their softer layers by water and wind. I see the rocks as beautiful and surprising in their forms. As a basic material of our planet, they are powerful and reassuring to me. They have a presence. I am fascinated by their appearance and love to draw them.

Knowing how I feel about these rocks helps me choose how to represent them. In my realistic portrayal of them I am asking the viewer to notice how extraordinary they are, how beautiful! I hope I can convey their power and nature's magnificent creativity. As I said in the poem, *I Love the Stories Rocks Tell*, "When I draw rocks I enter the timeless mystery of creation and find my place in the Universe".

Part 1
The Process

Finding the subject

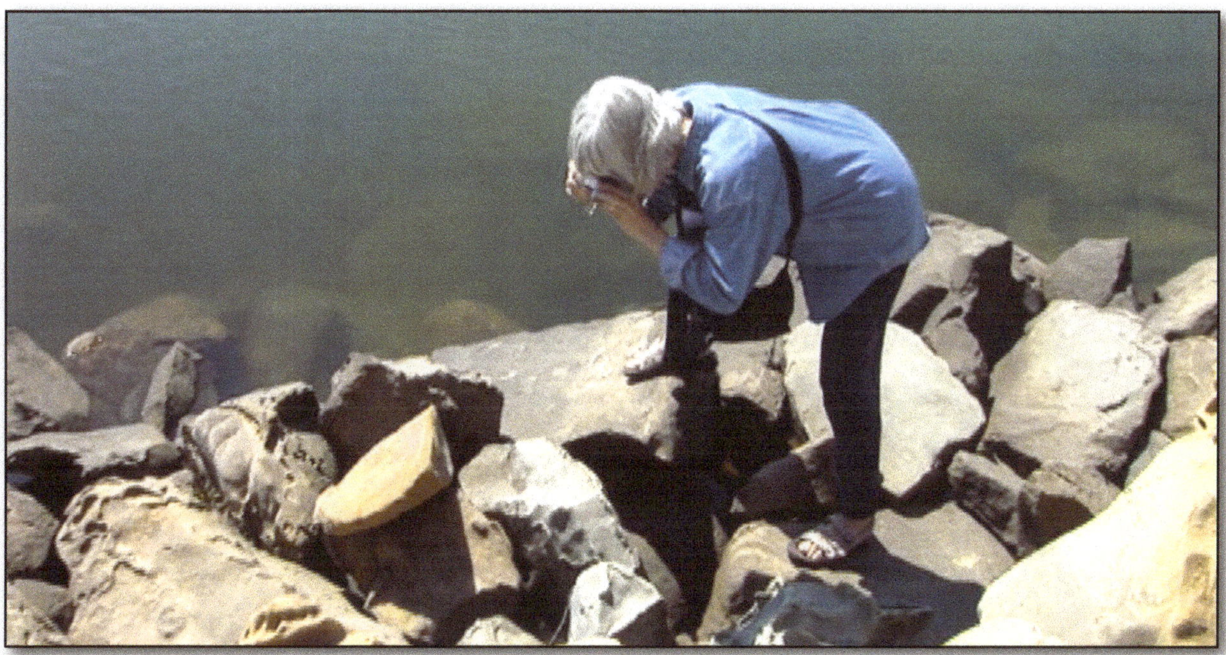

On a field trip I gather information. I take many pictures, not knowing which ones might be useful in my drawing. I look for images with interesting shapes, a clear interplay of light and shadow, or an arresting gesture. The entire drawing depends upon this critical first step.

A Choice is Made

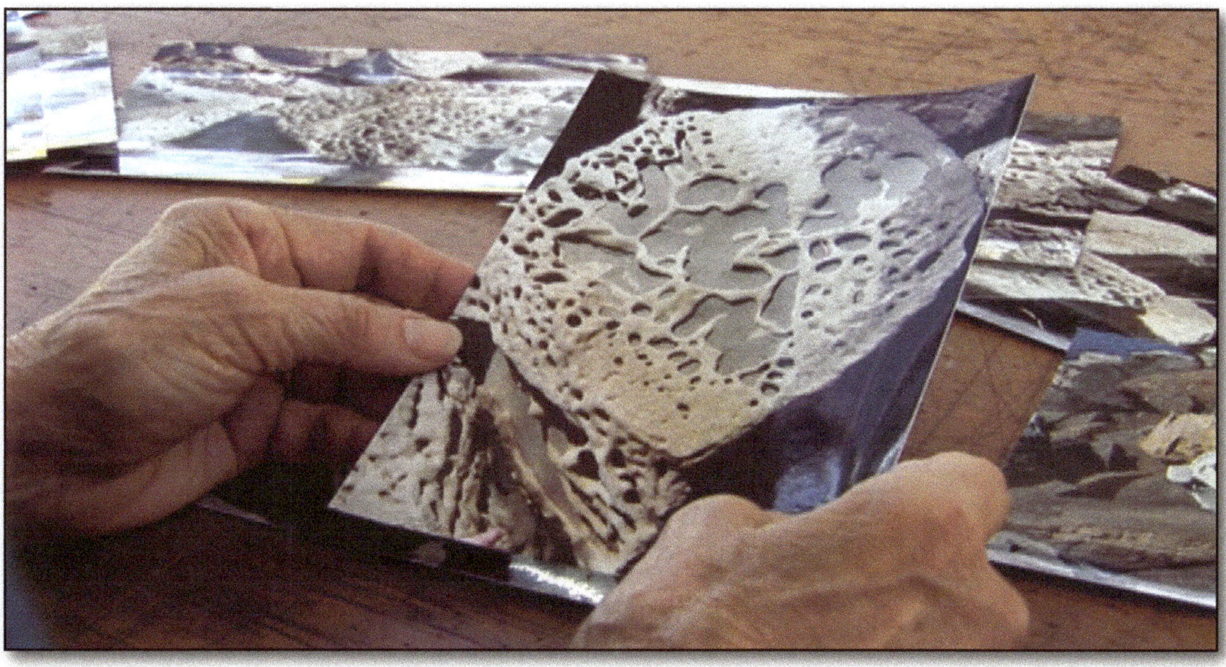

This rock struck me as having a particularly strong presence.

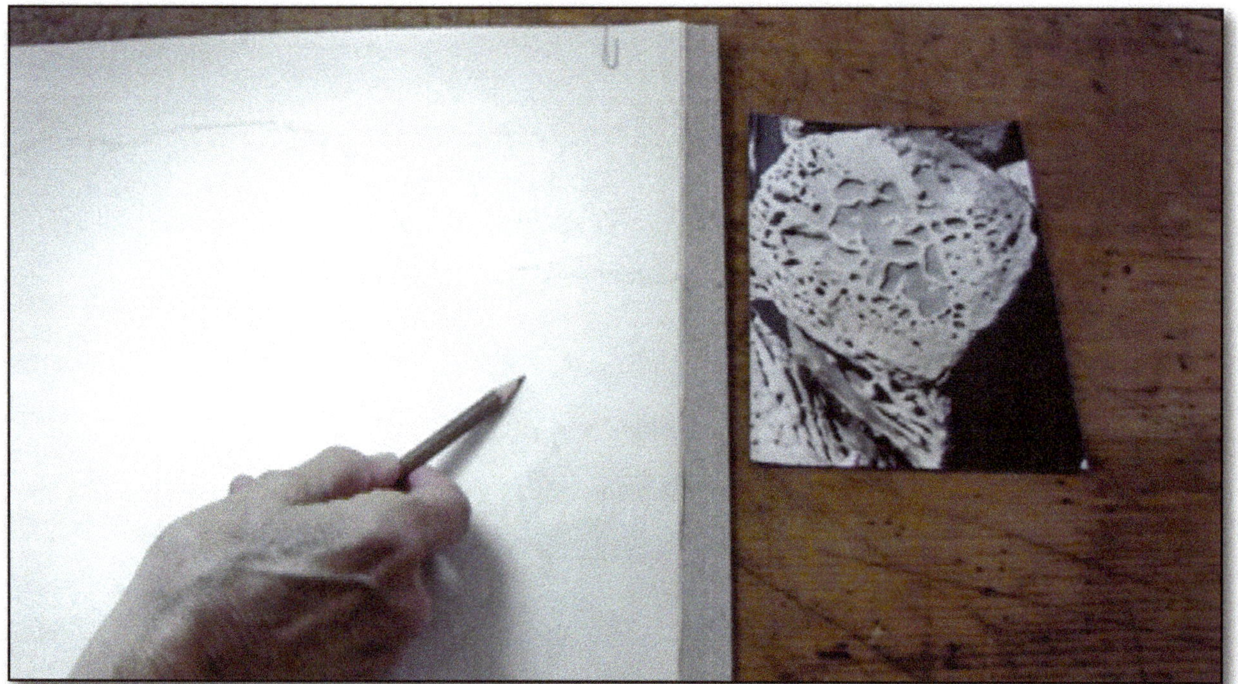

First, I freehand sketch the rock on to newsprint - looking for overall shape, size, how parts are related to each other and the whole, and where to place things on the page. The major features of the rock are the focus at this time. As I work, my eye is becoming more and more familiar with the image - I begin to learn what this rock really looks like.

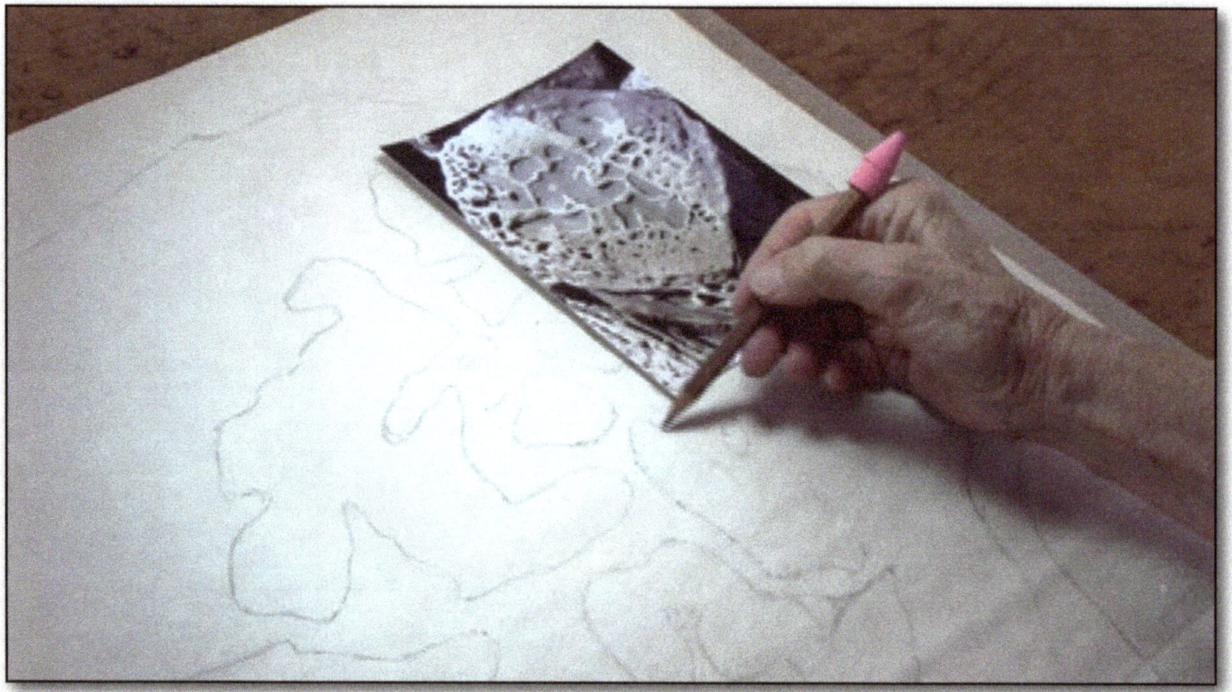

Once the overall placement is established I focus on the inner details of each section - each shape is unique and all are interrelated to one another.

Outline, proportion and position are particularly important.

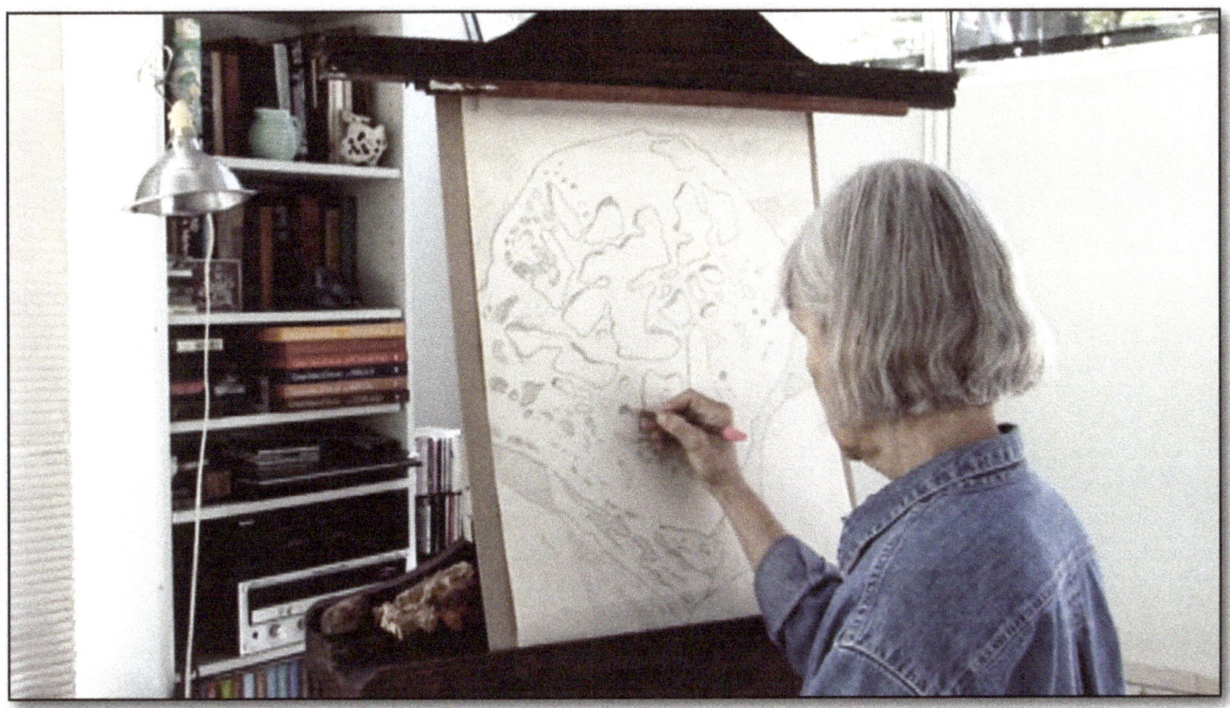

I begin to develop shadow patterns of darks and lights - main elements of the composition.

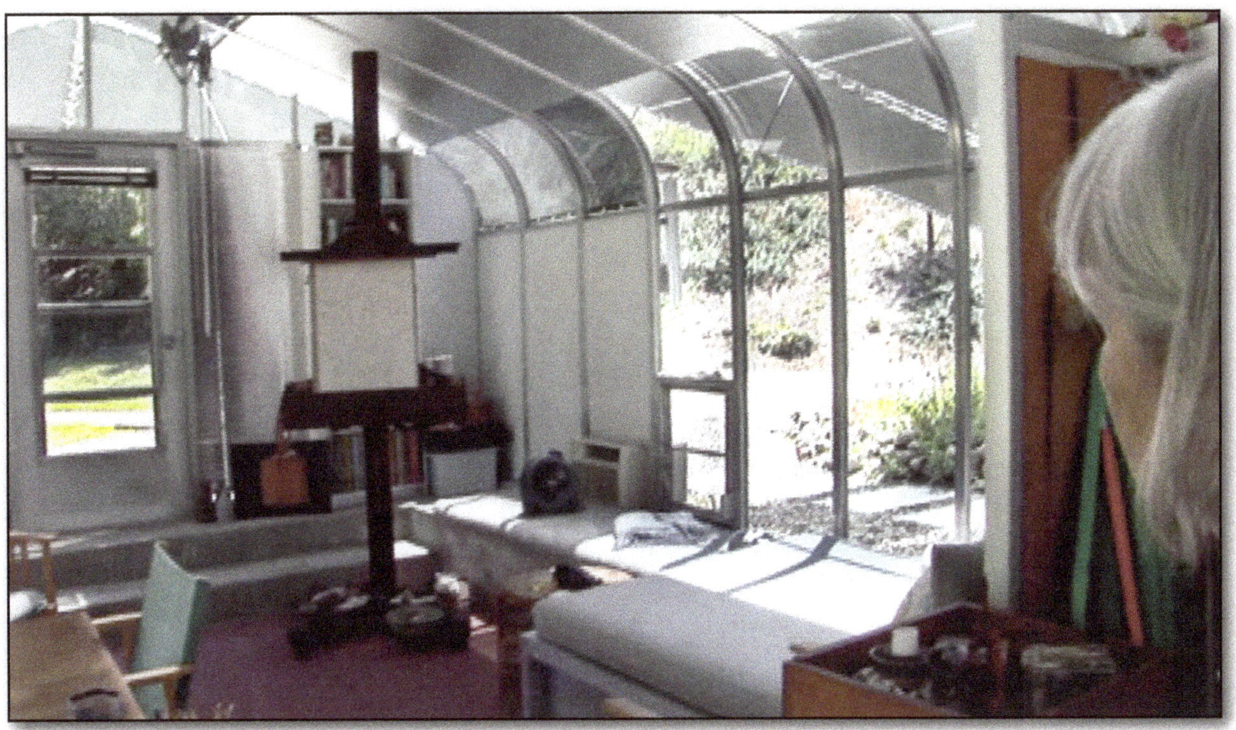

Walking back and viewing from a distance helps me to keep the whole and the parts properly related.

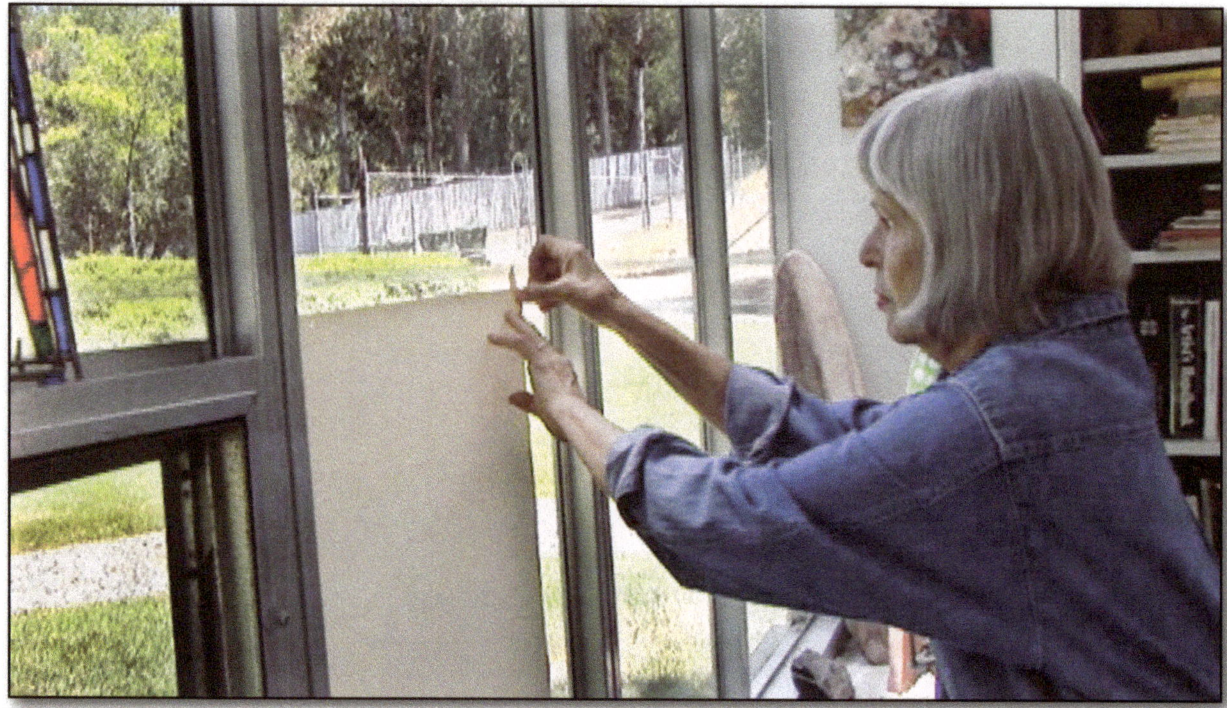

To transfer this rough sketch to the final drawing paper I must turn the page over, find a source of light to shine through the paper, and color over the lines on the back side of the paper.

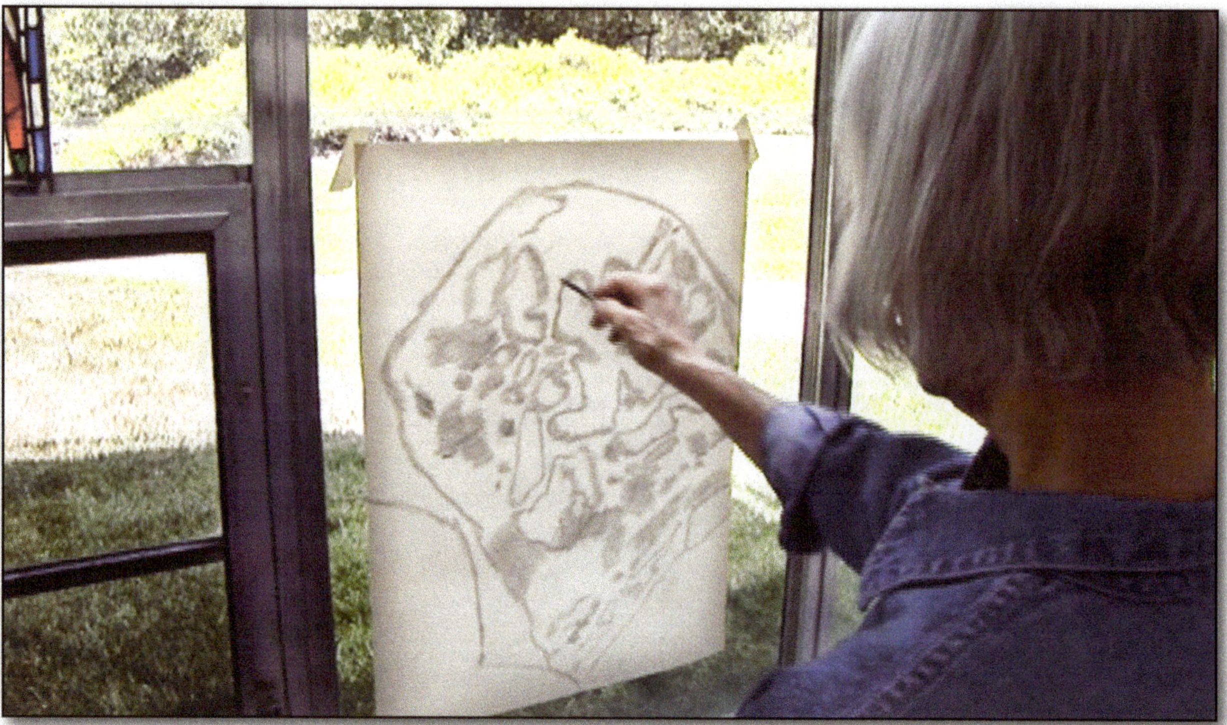

I use a fat piece of graphite for this. I turn the page over and check to be sure I've colored all the lines.

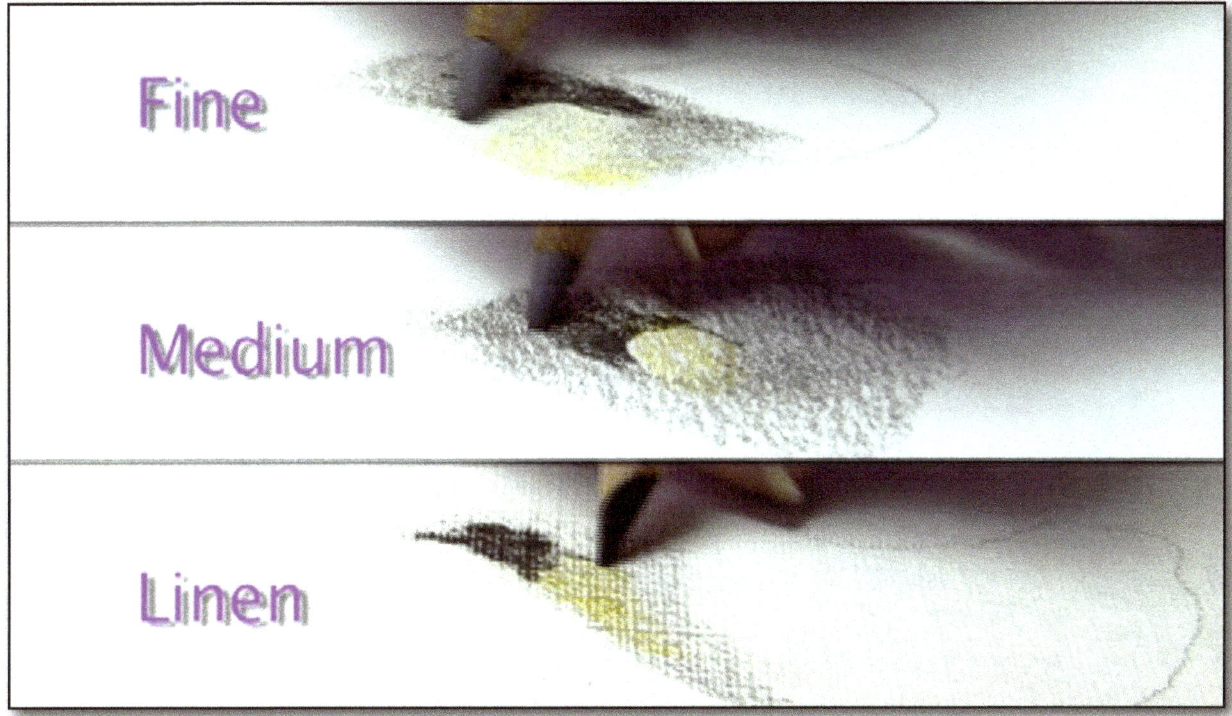

Finding the right texture for the paper is another critical step. Drawing with a Prismacolor pencil on some test pieces will bring out the textures and enable me to make a choice.

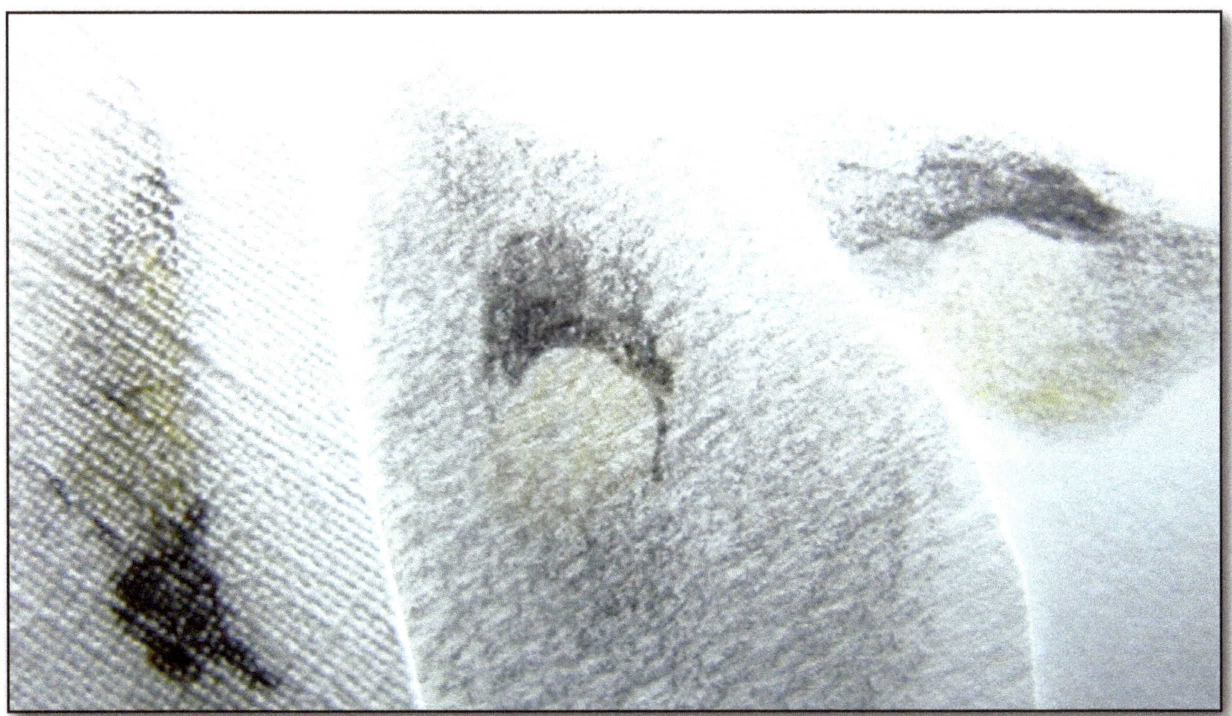

In this case, the finer textured paper matches more closely the fine textures of the rocks.

Attaching the Paper to a Backing

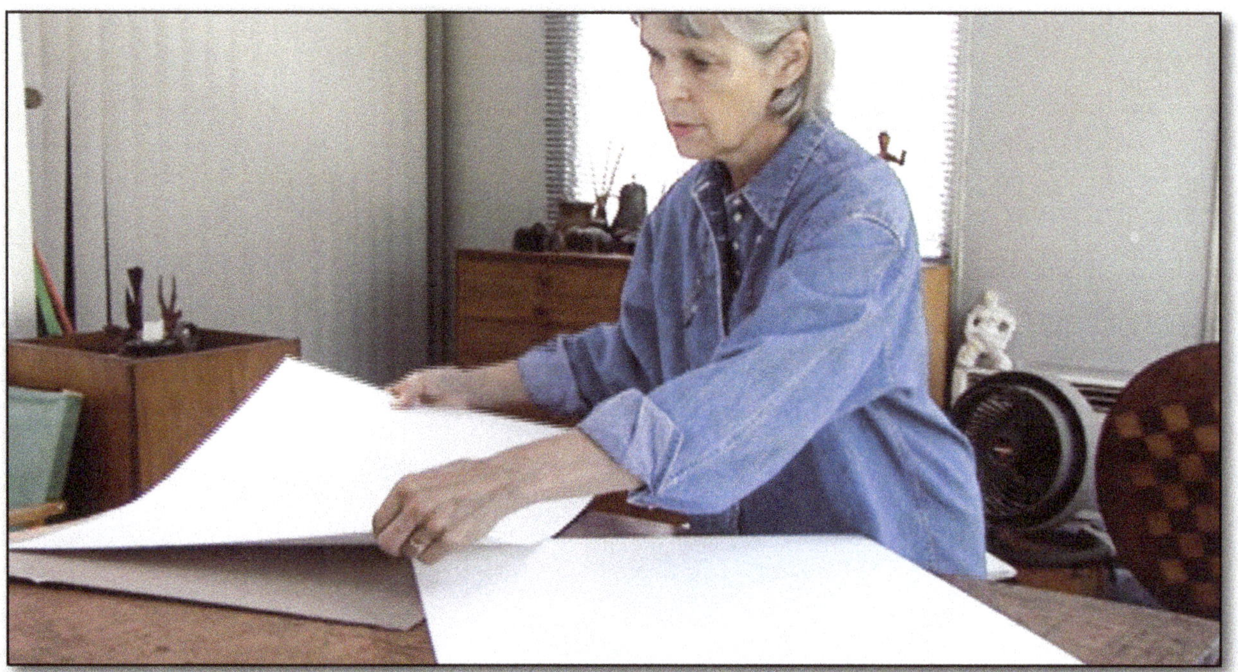

It will help if the drawing paper can be stiffened so that it is protected from folds, bent corners, and can be propped up on my easel for viewing.

Transferring the Sketch

Next, I transfer the rough sketch to the paper.

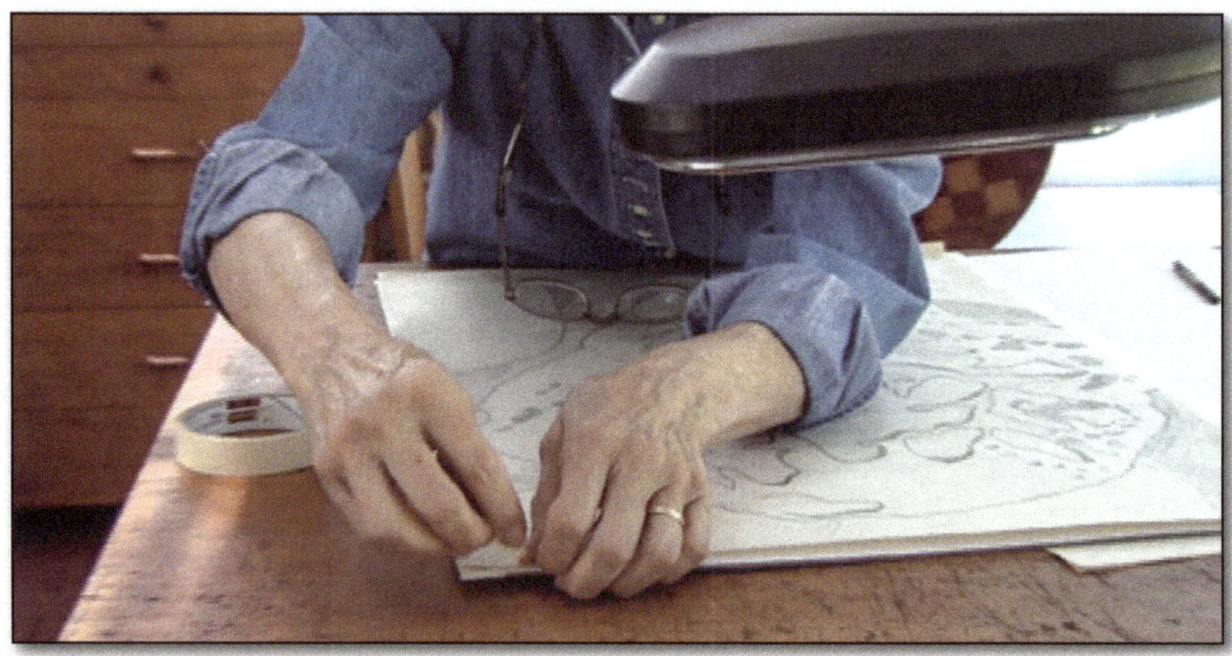

It's important that the sketch does not move during this process. I tape it in place.

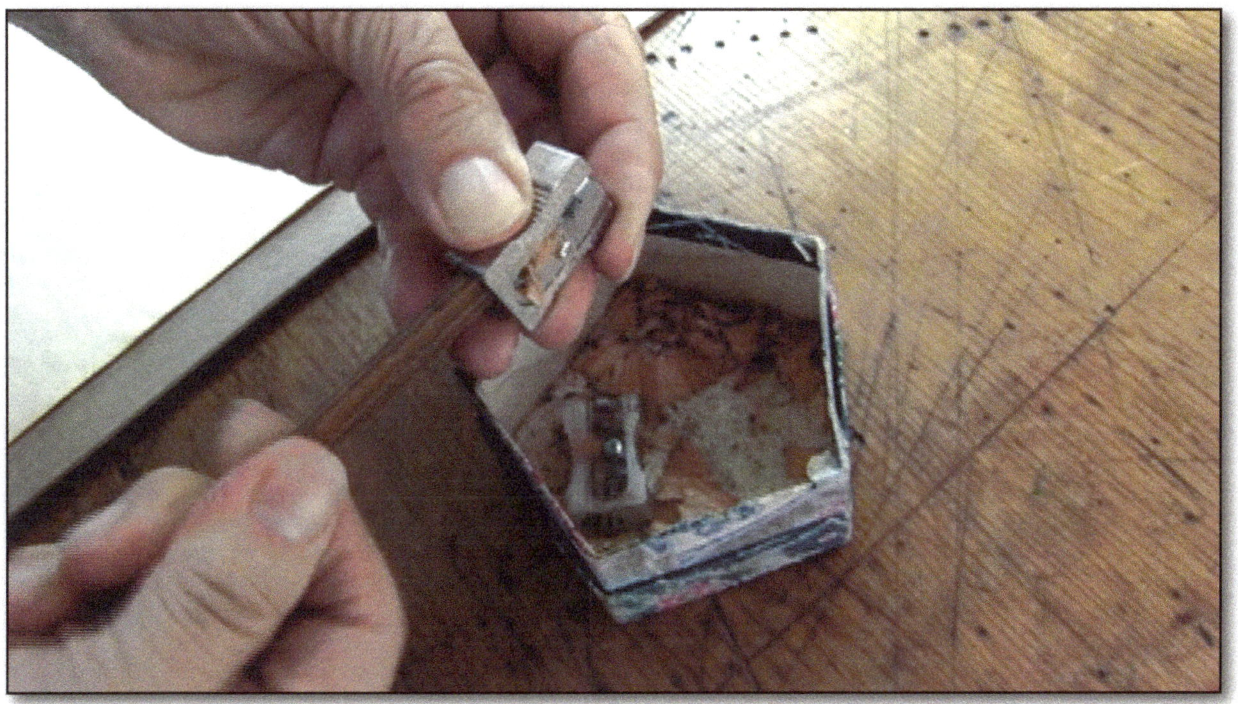

A very sharp pencil helps when tracing the lines of the sketch onto the paper.

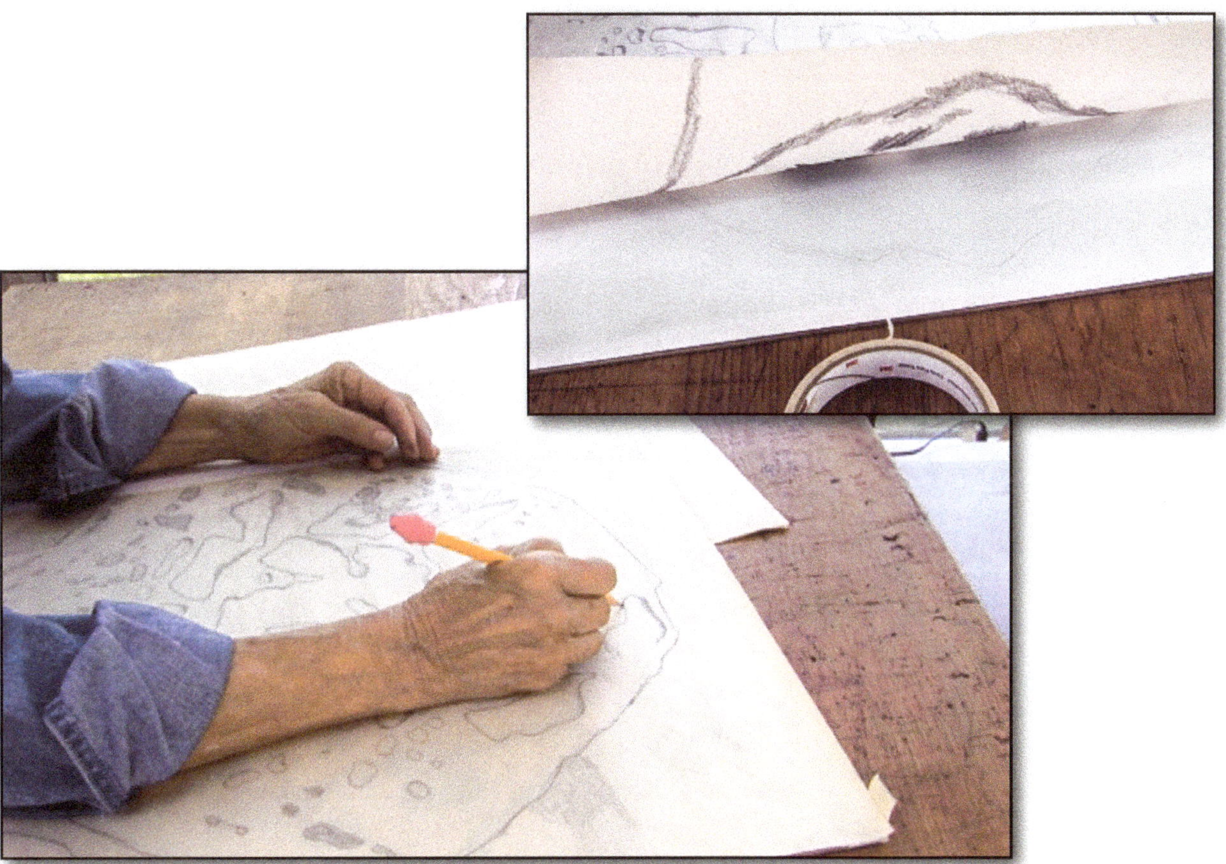

The resulting lines will be very light and need to be traced over again on the final sheet.

Underlying Color

Once the basic outline of the drawing is established, the coloring can begin.

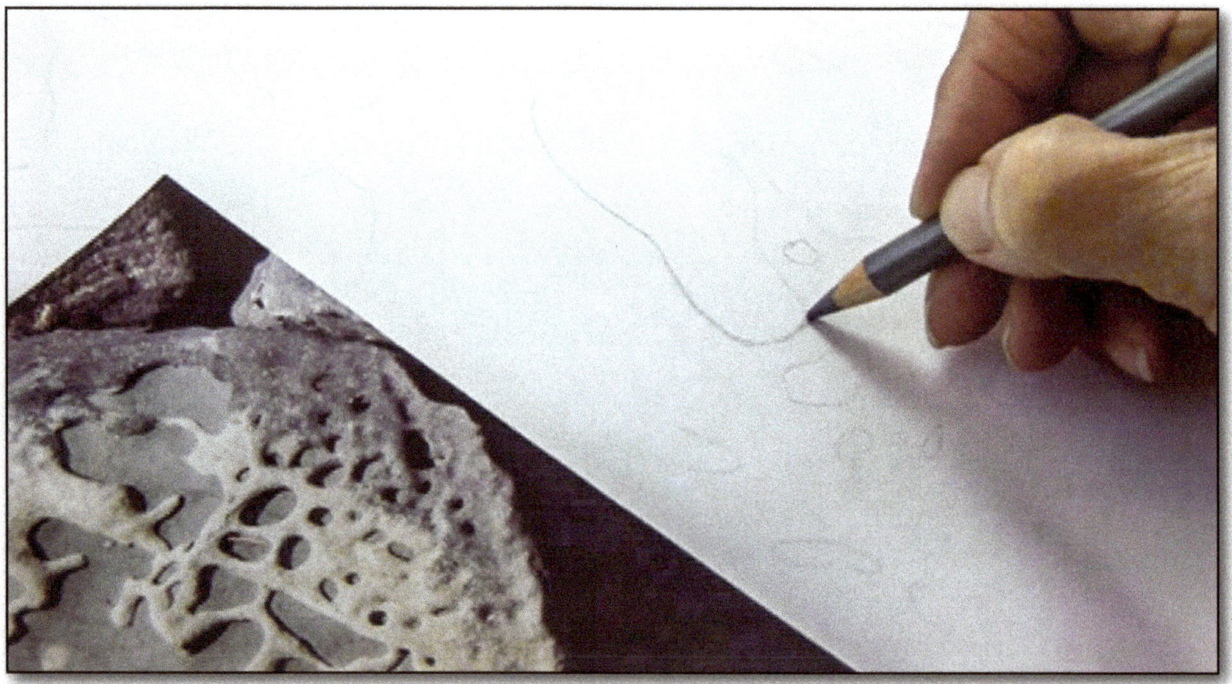

Underlying color can be very different than the final over layers of color.

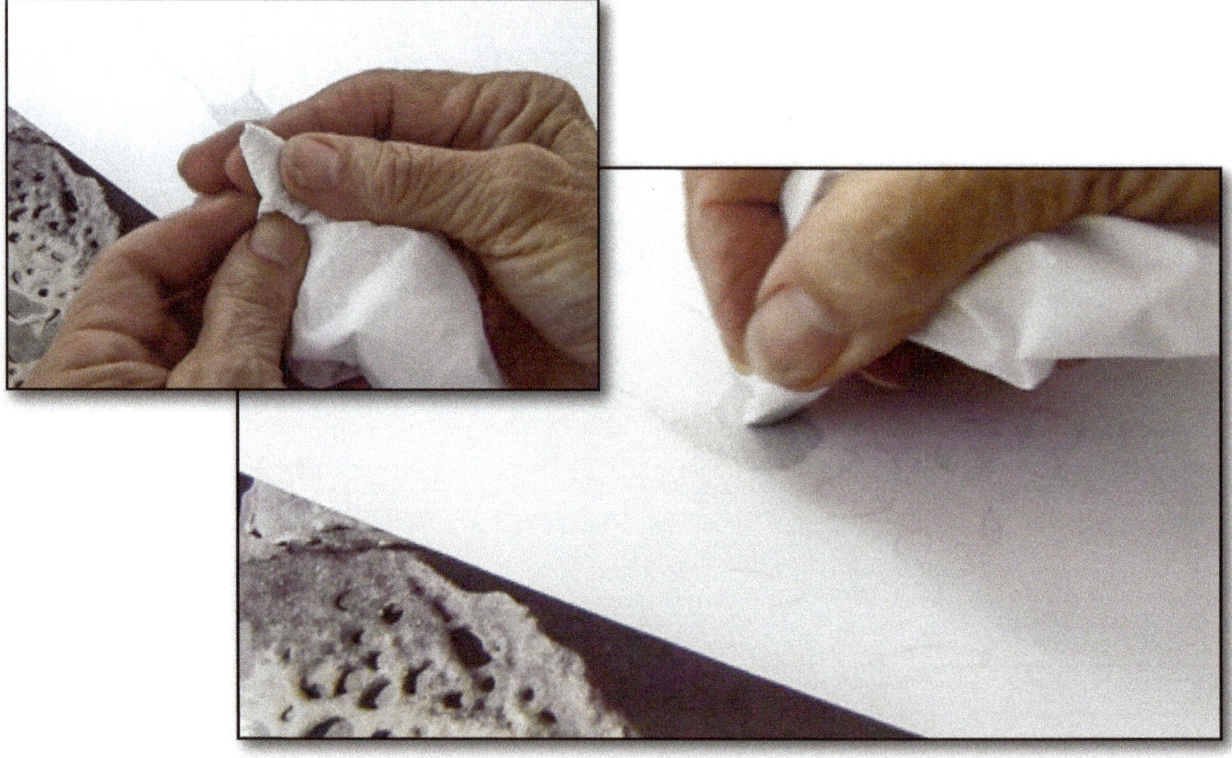

They can be rubbed in to fill the white pours of the paper. I use a folded tissue for this.

White areas must be left white to start with, as it is extremely difficult to get back to white once color has been applied.

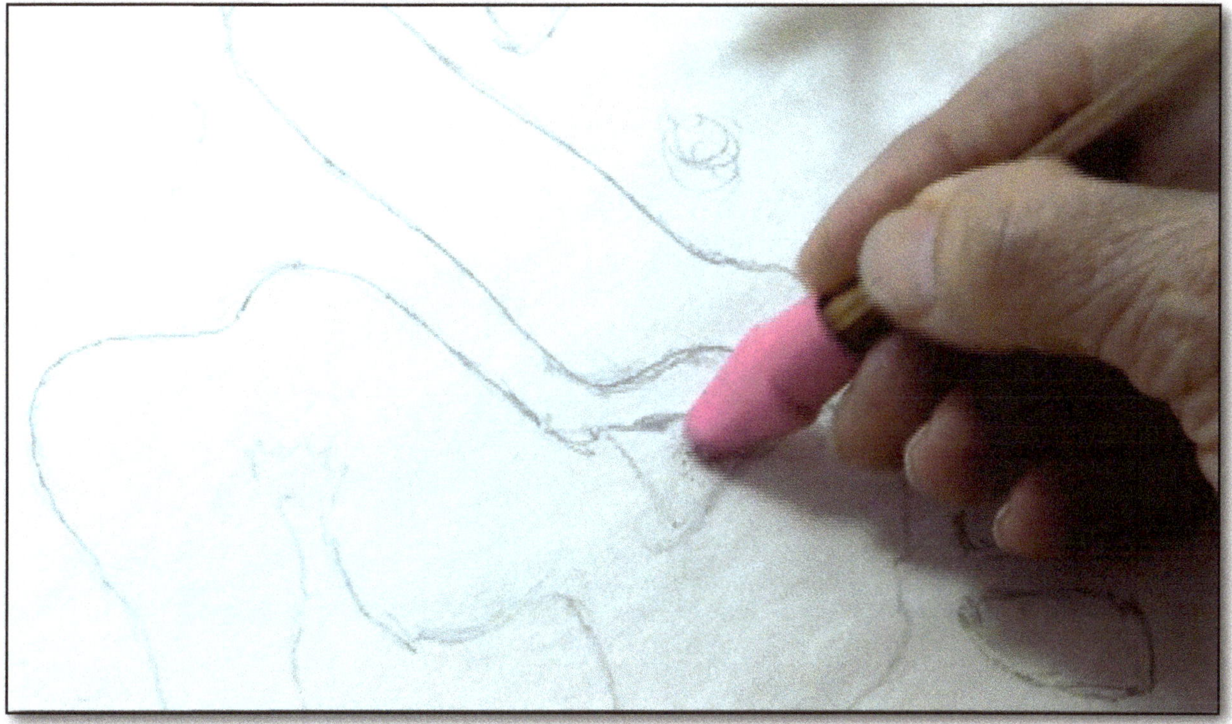

I frequently use the eraser not only to clean up areas as I go but also to define outlines and pick up highlights.

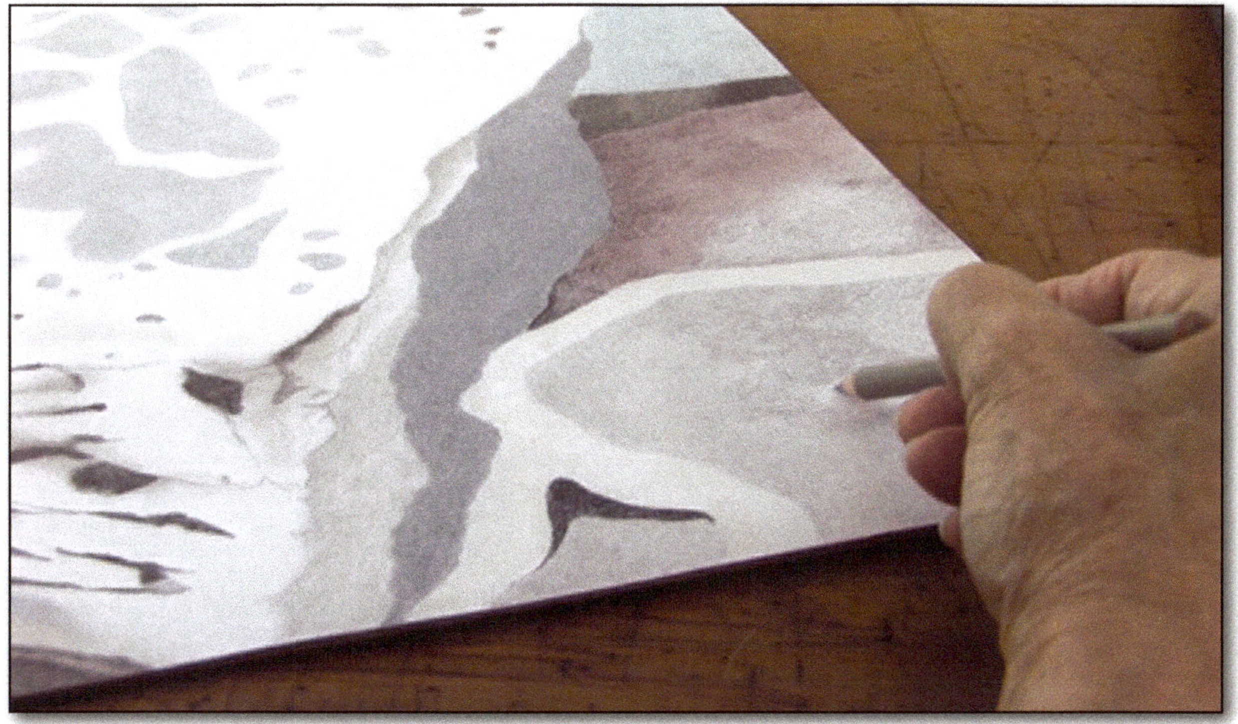

It takes many hours to pencil in this all-important layer of color. The underlying colors will influence all of my colors drawn over them.

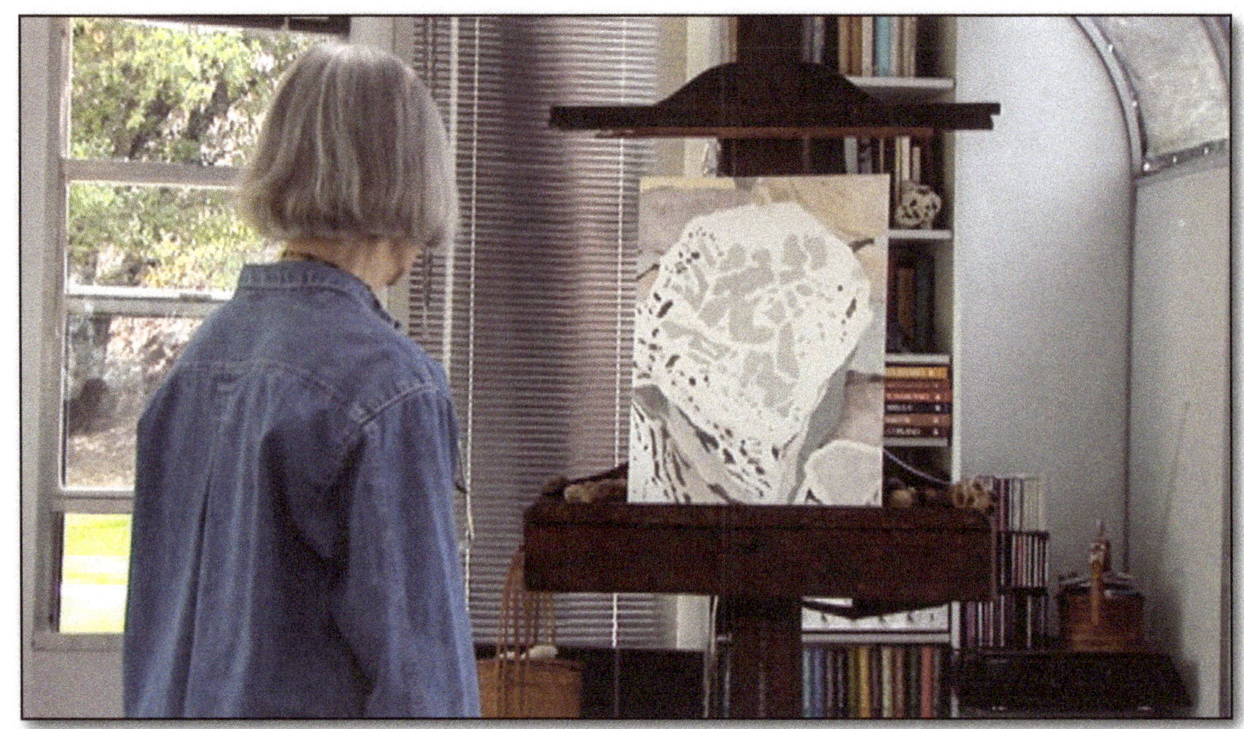

<h1 style="text-align:center">Overlays of Color</h1>

Before I use them on the drawing, I experiment with overlays of color to see what affects I can achieve.

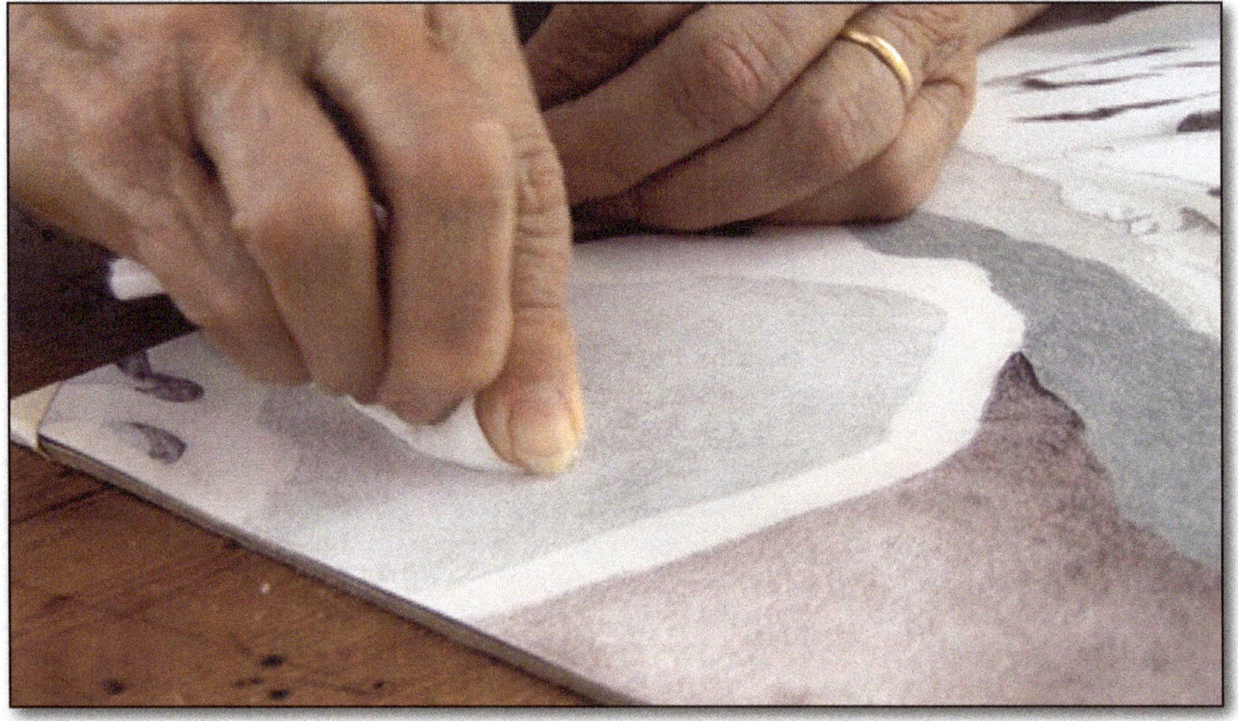

Rubbing over layers into under layers can blend colors, or they can be left as texture.

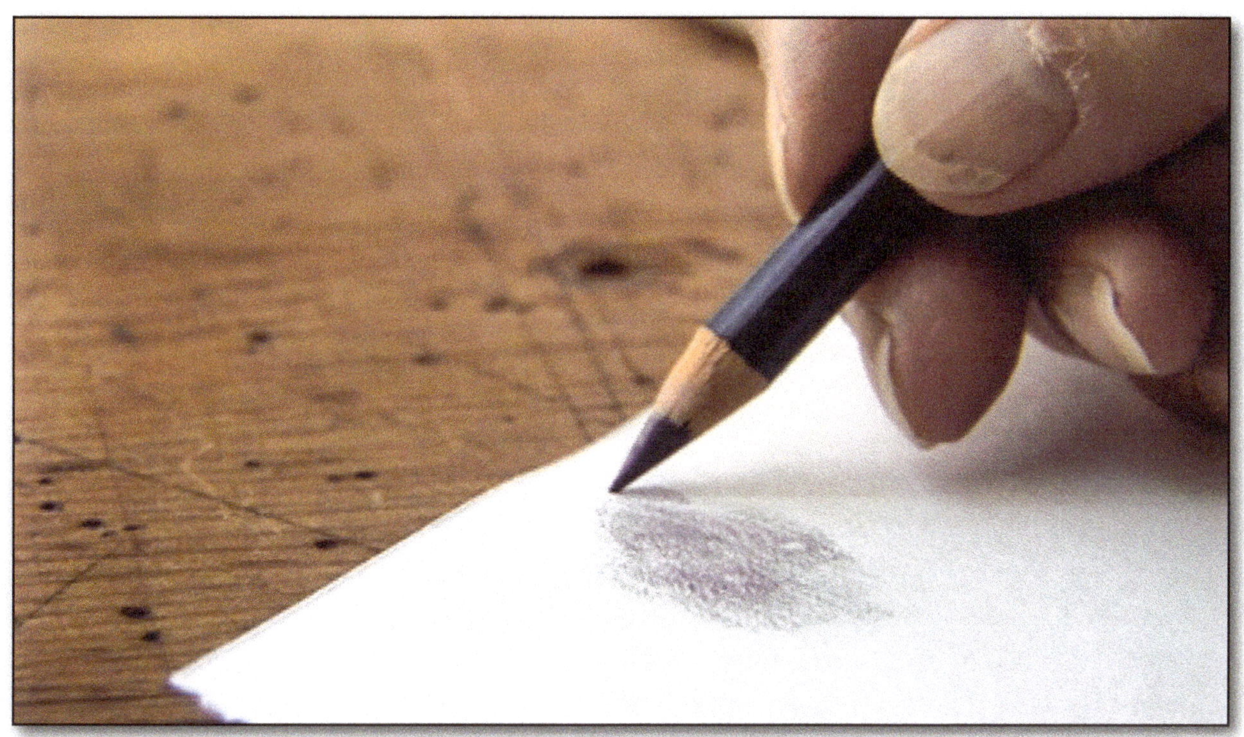

Here I experiment with grape over cool light grey before I apply it to my drawing.

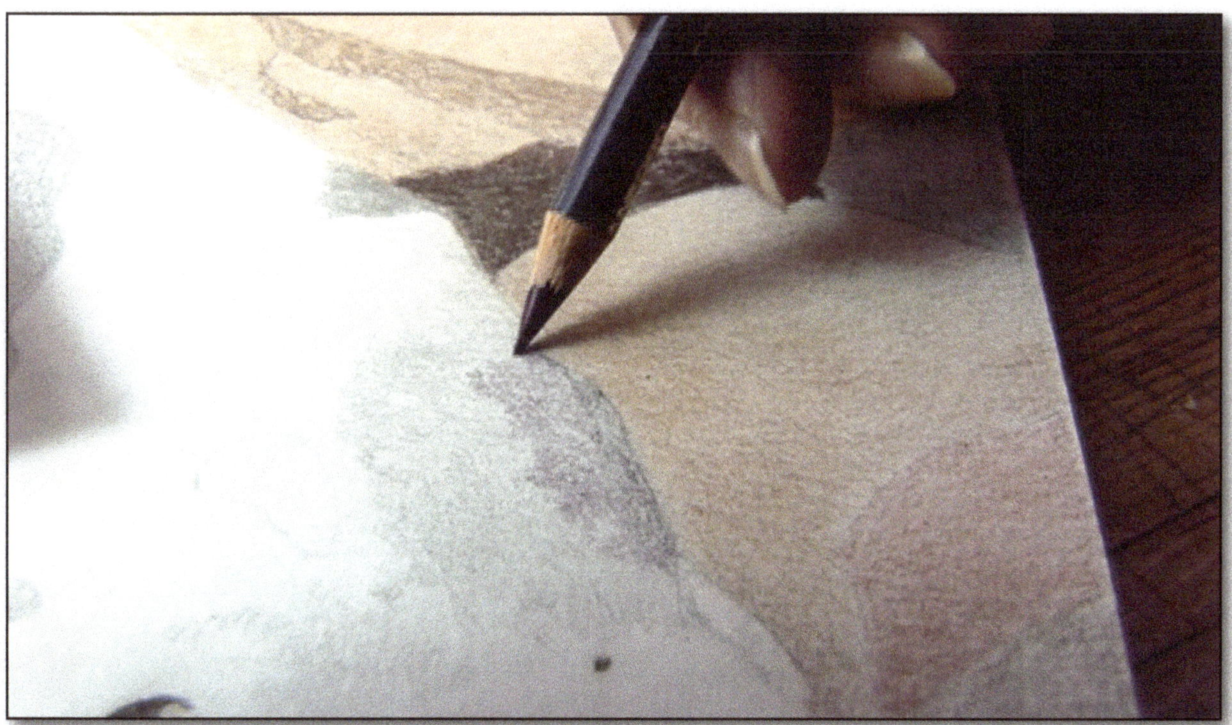

I apply the grape color and do not rub it to create the grainy texture of the rock. Notice how I am drawing the darker overlying color to define the light spot which is left alone.

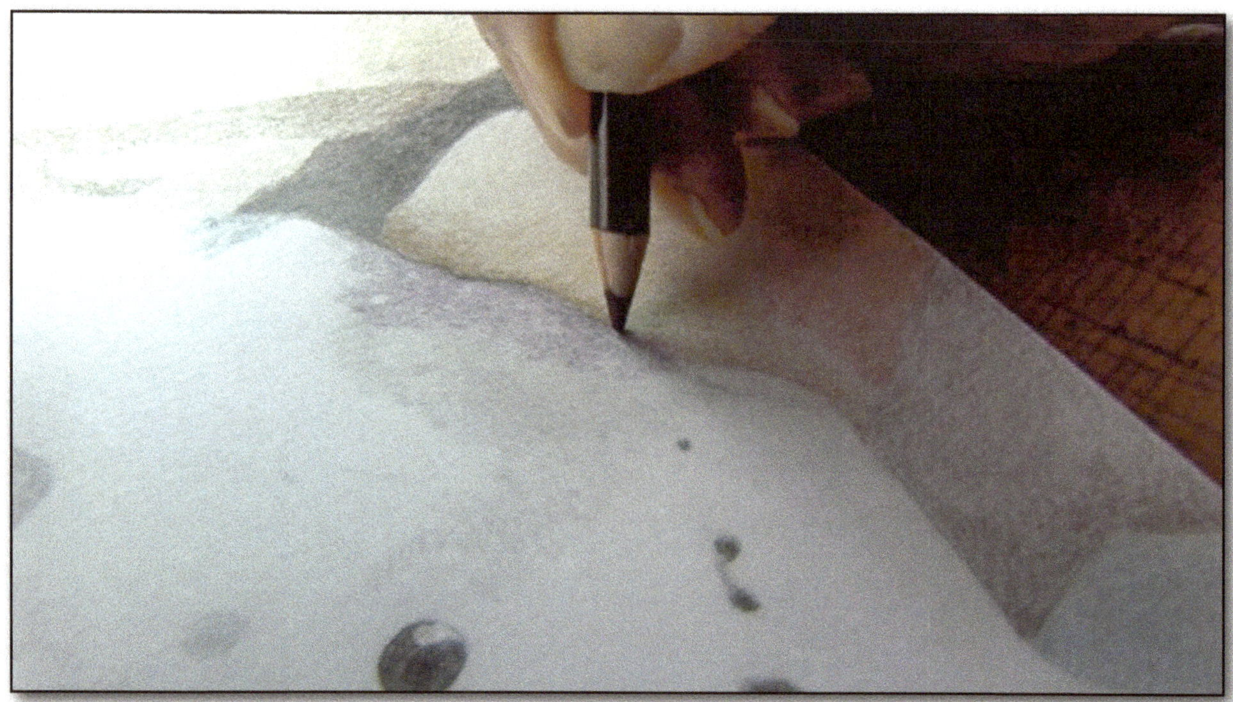

Defining borders will give the final drawing its focused appearance. I take one section at a time and work each very carefully.

Shadow Lines - Creating Dimension

Creating the shadow lines will give the rock surface its three dimensional appearance.

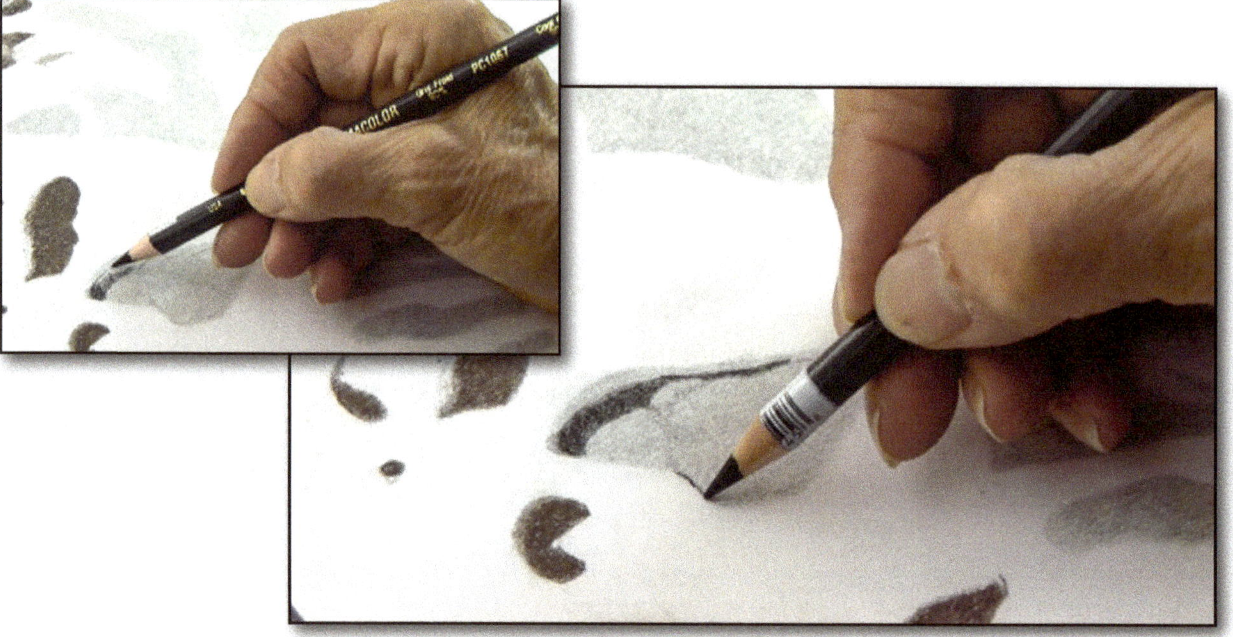

Darker colors require a heavier pressure. Once in place they are very difficult to erase.

The process of drawing may seem slow, but I prefer to think of it as thoughtful, wonderful and caring - each moment savored for its feeling of calm and intention.

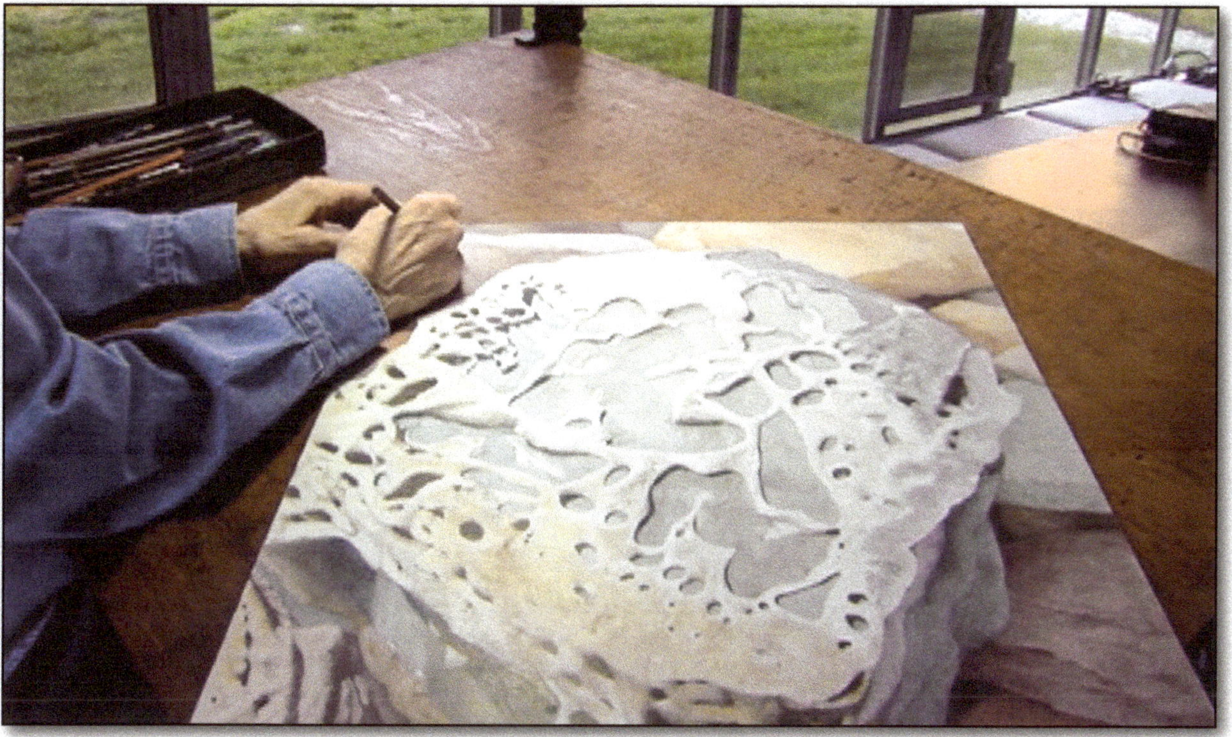

Eventually, every section has been carefully drawn - always keeping the whole in mind.

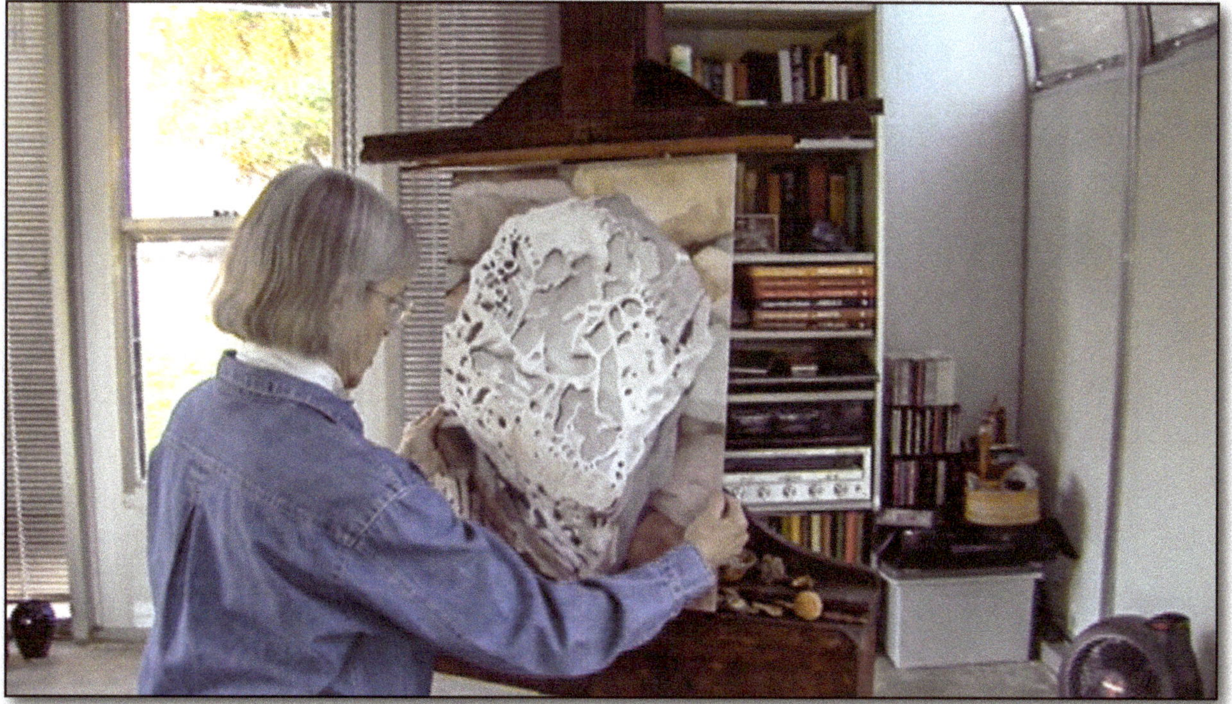

The final critical step is to take a long view and pull everything together.

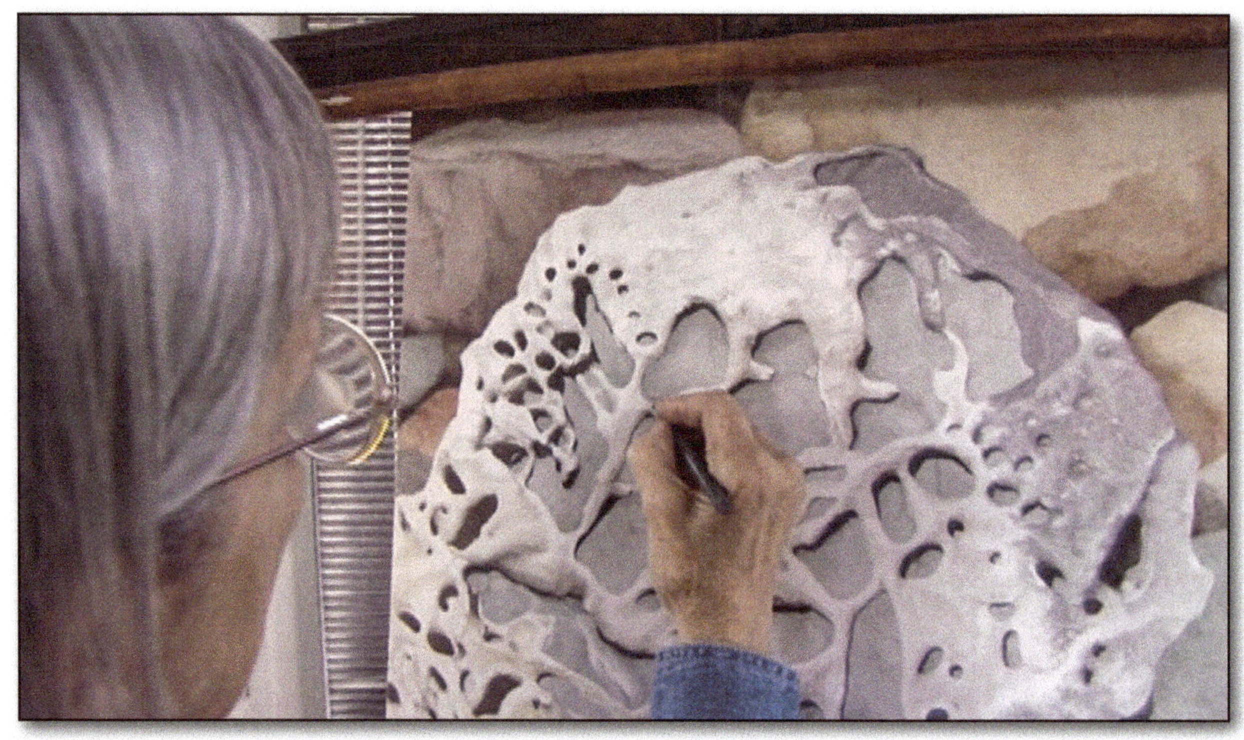

Details are strengthened, highlights and shadows intensified, colors adjusted...

Until the drawing Sings!

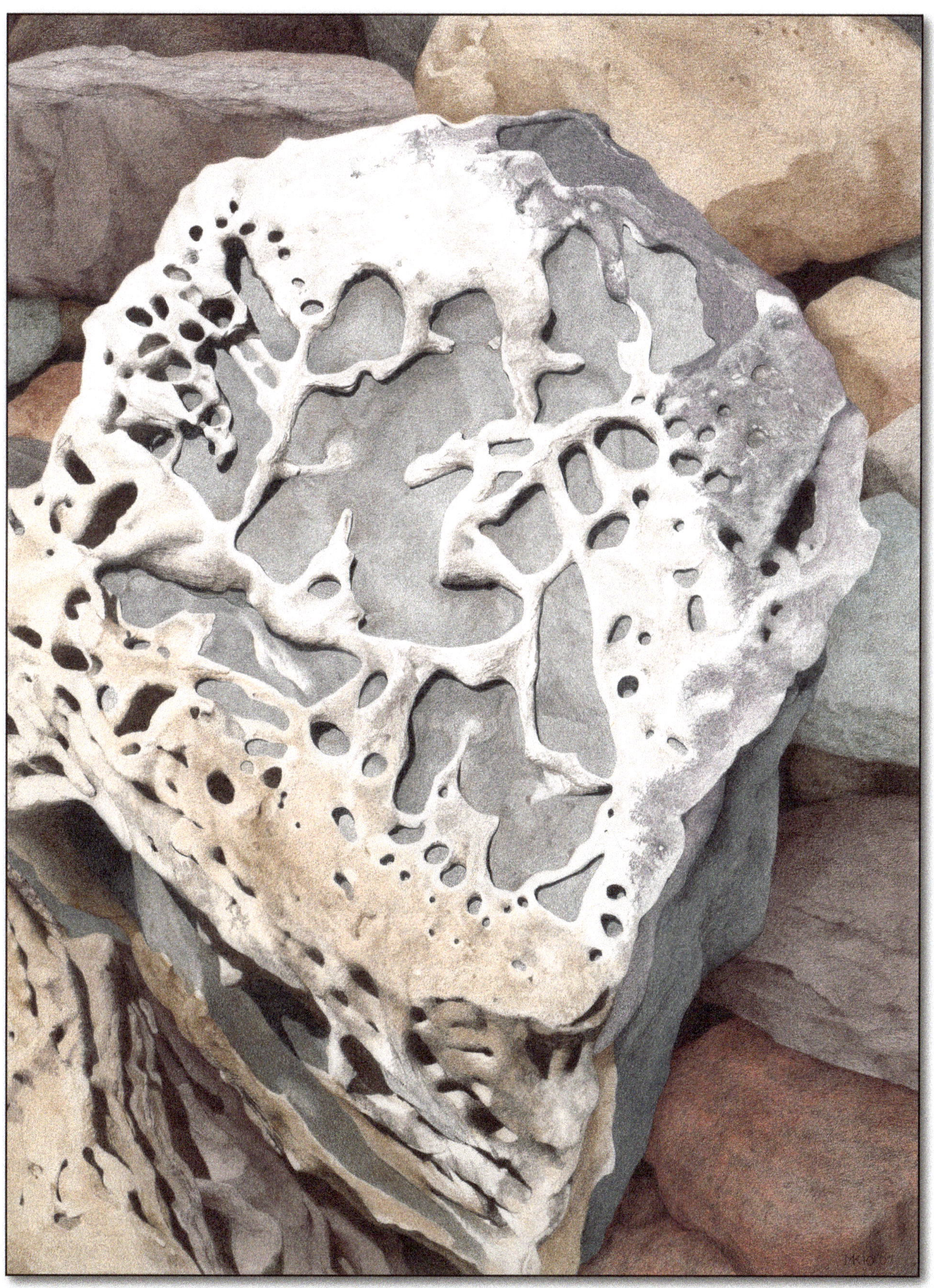

Part 2
The Artwork

At The Waters Edge

There is something tantalizing about the waters edge.

Standing on the shore we watch the land gradually disappear into the mysterious realm of the sea. The sky reflected on the water's surface obscures what lies beneath.

The water rising and falling reveals and conceals, distorts and magnifies, intensifies and blurs.

The rocks find their power in standing firm against the constant ebb and flow, even as they are slowly eroded into natural sculpture, beautiful in their diversity and surprising configurations.

When I draw this transition, the place where two worlds meet and crossover, I feel the eternal forces of nature and know a timeless universe.

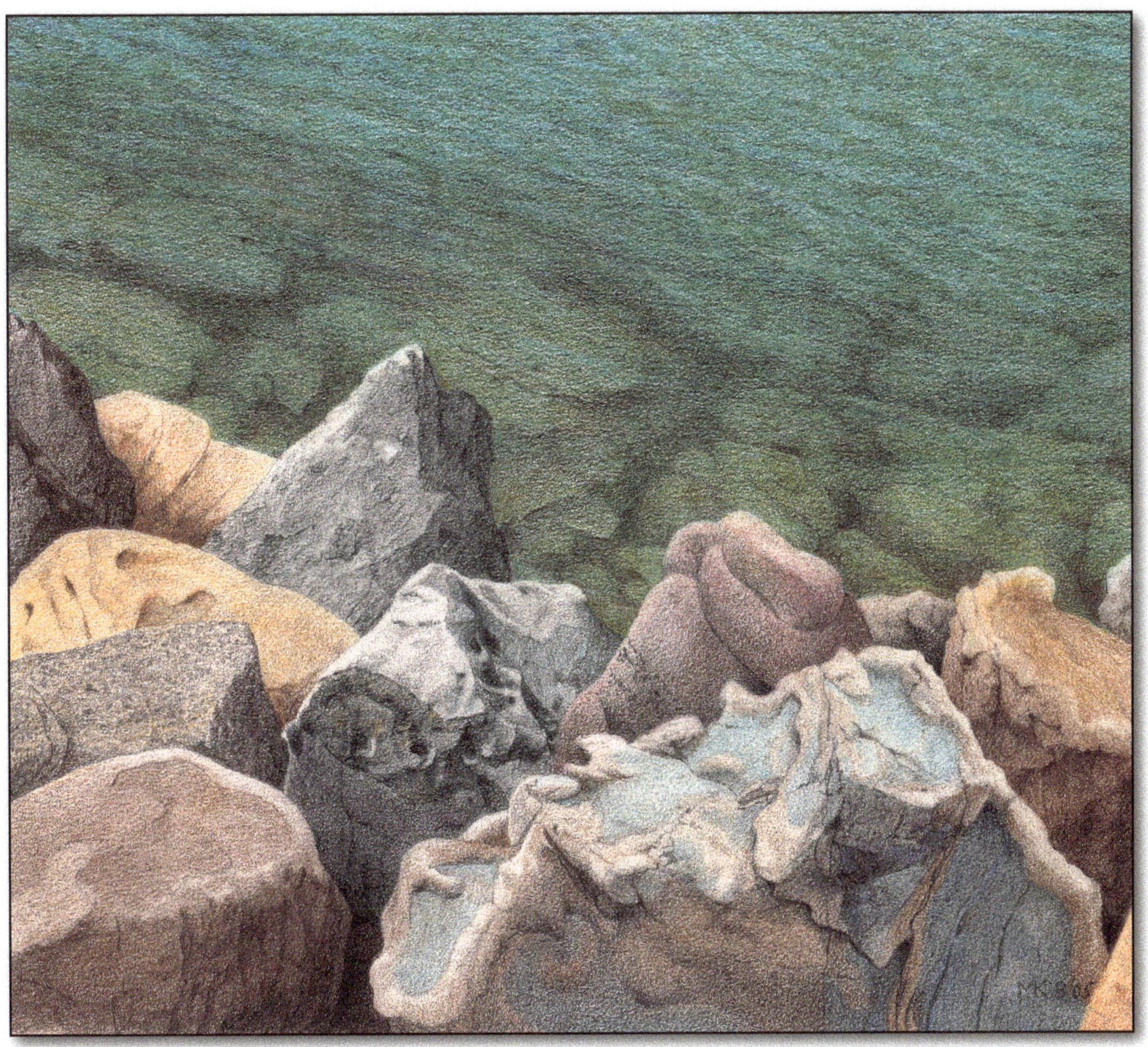

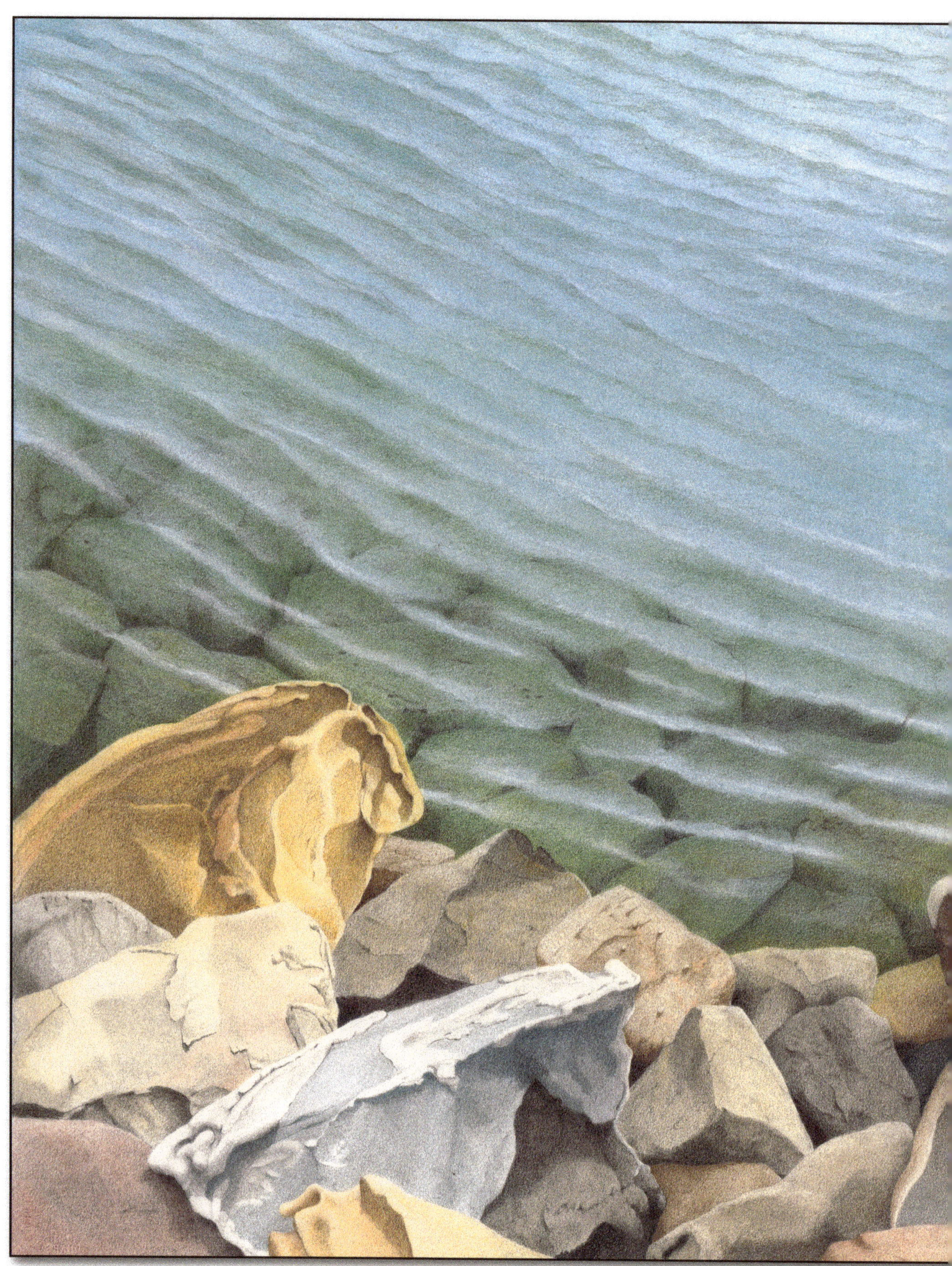

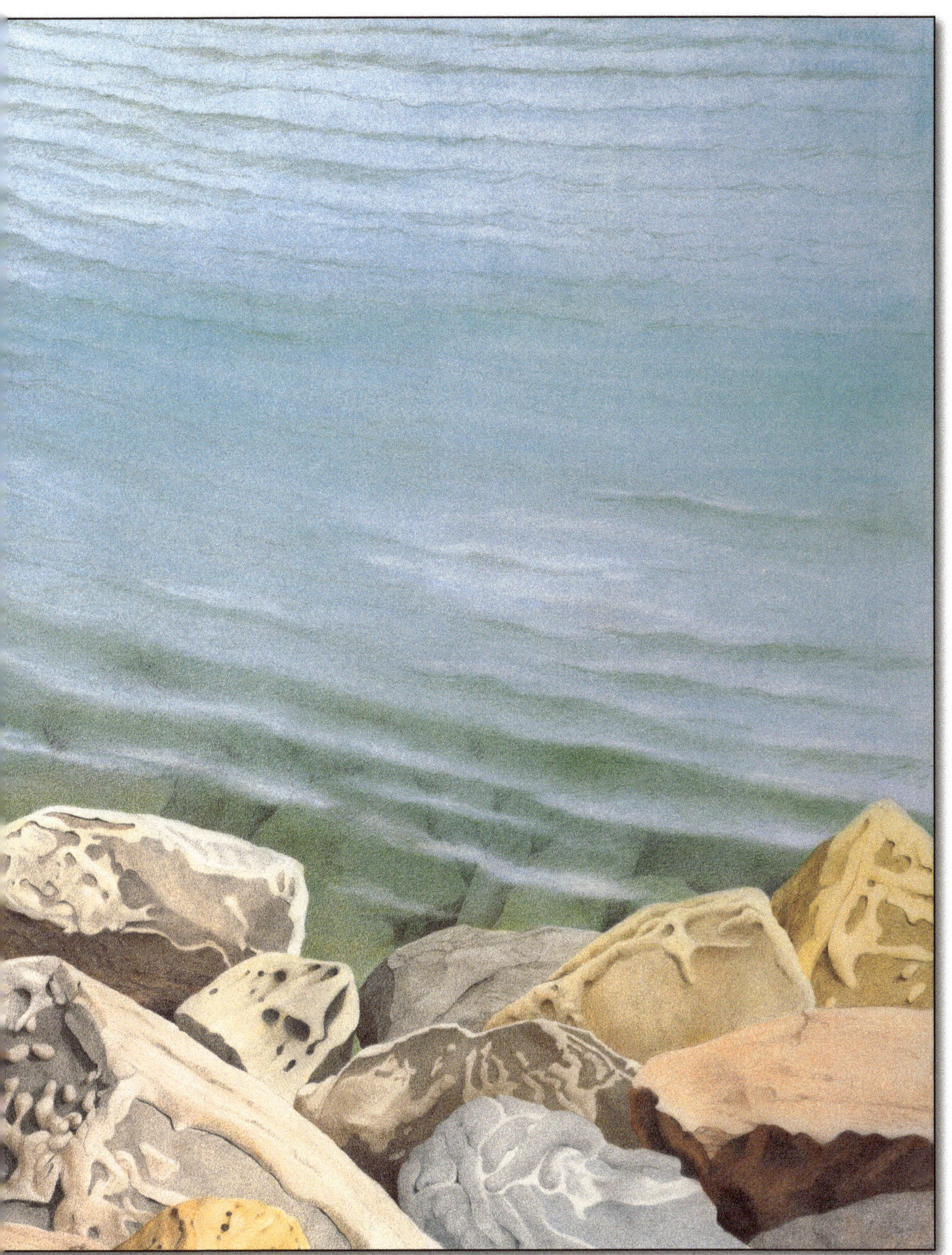

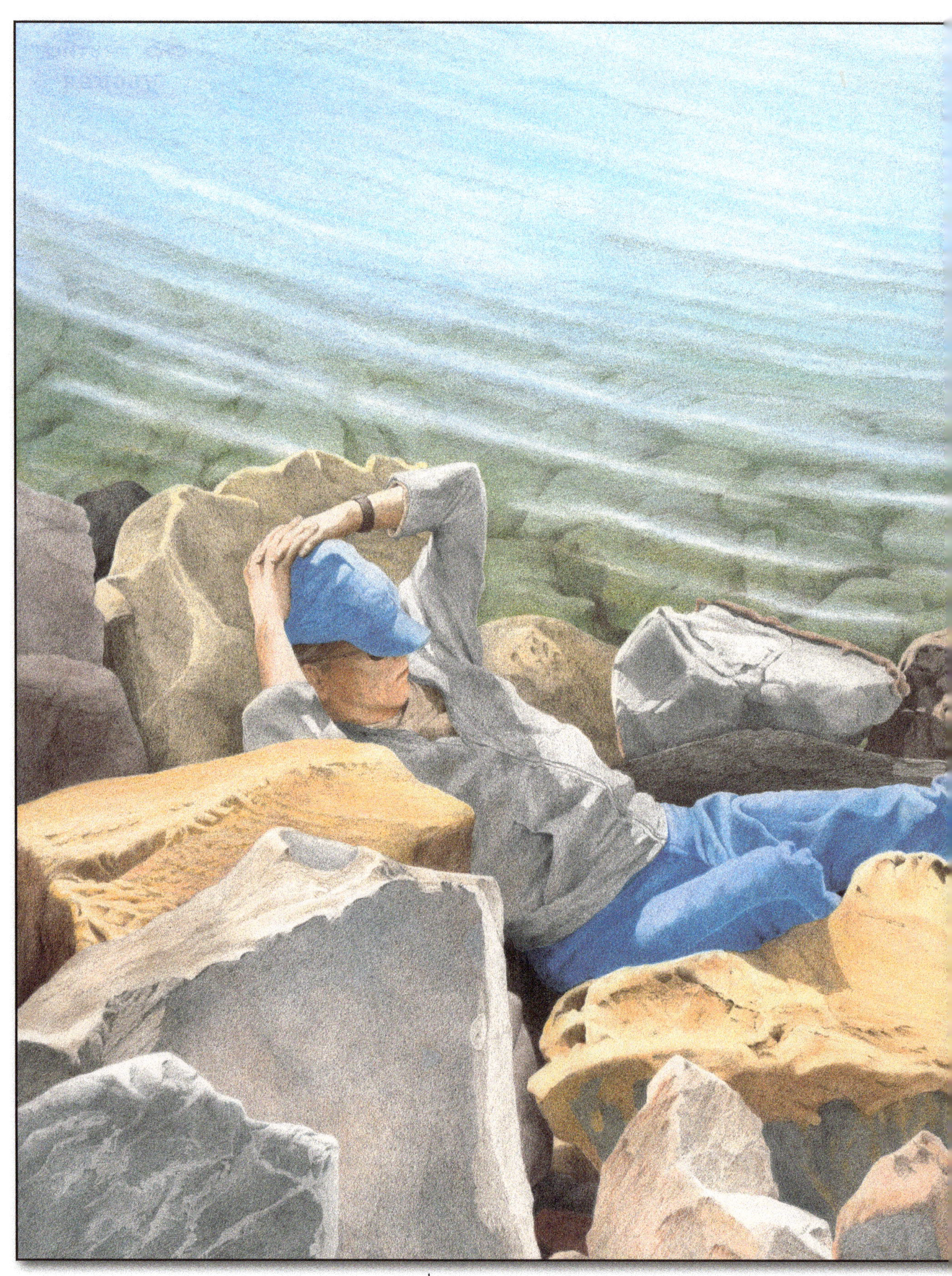

Time Out - 26" x 41"

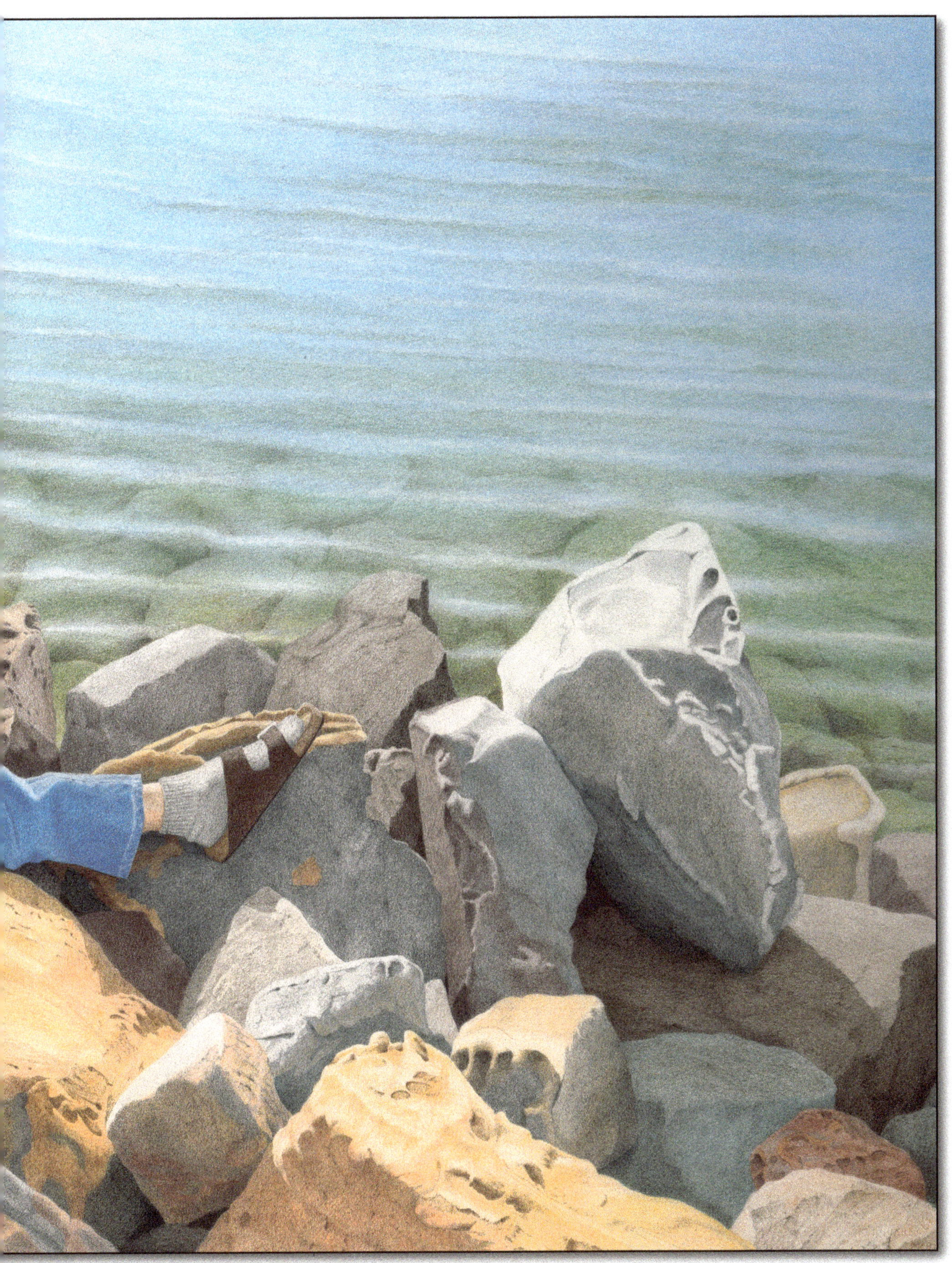

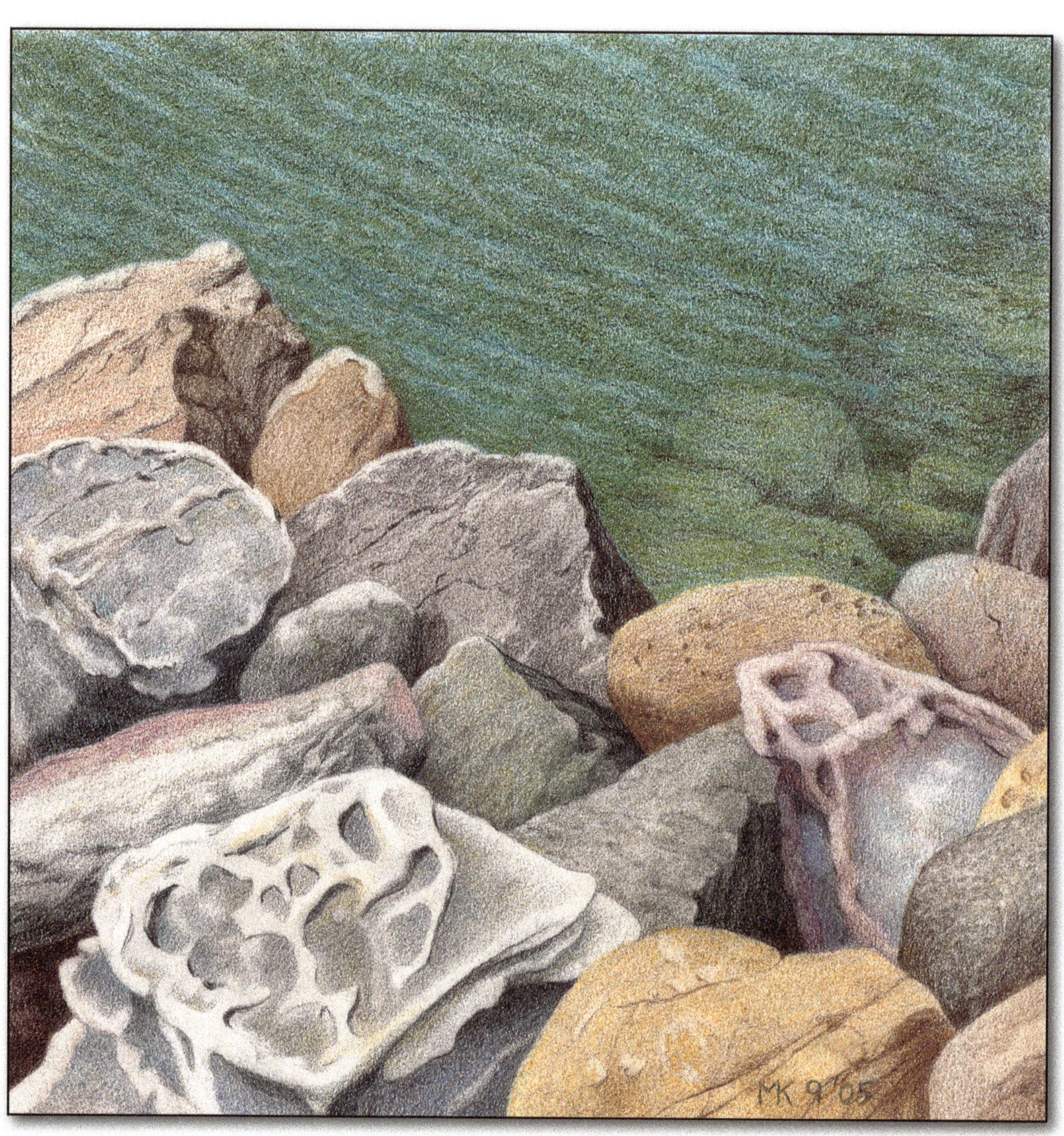

MK 9 '65

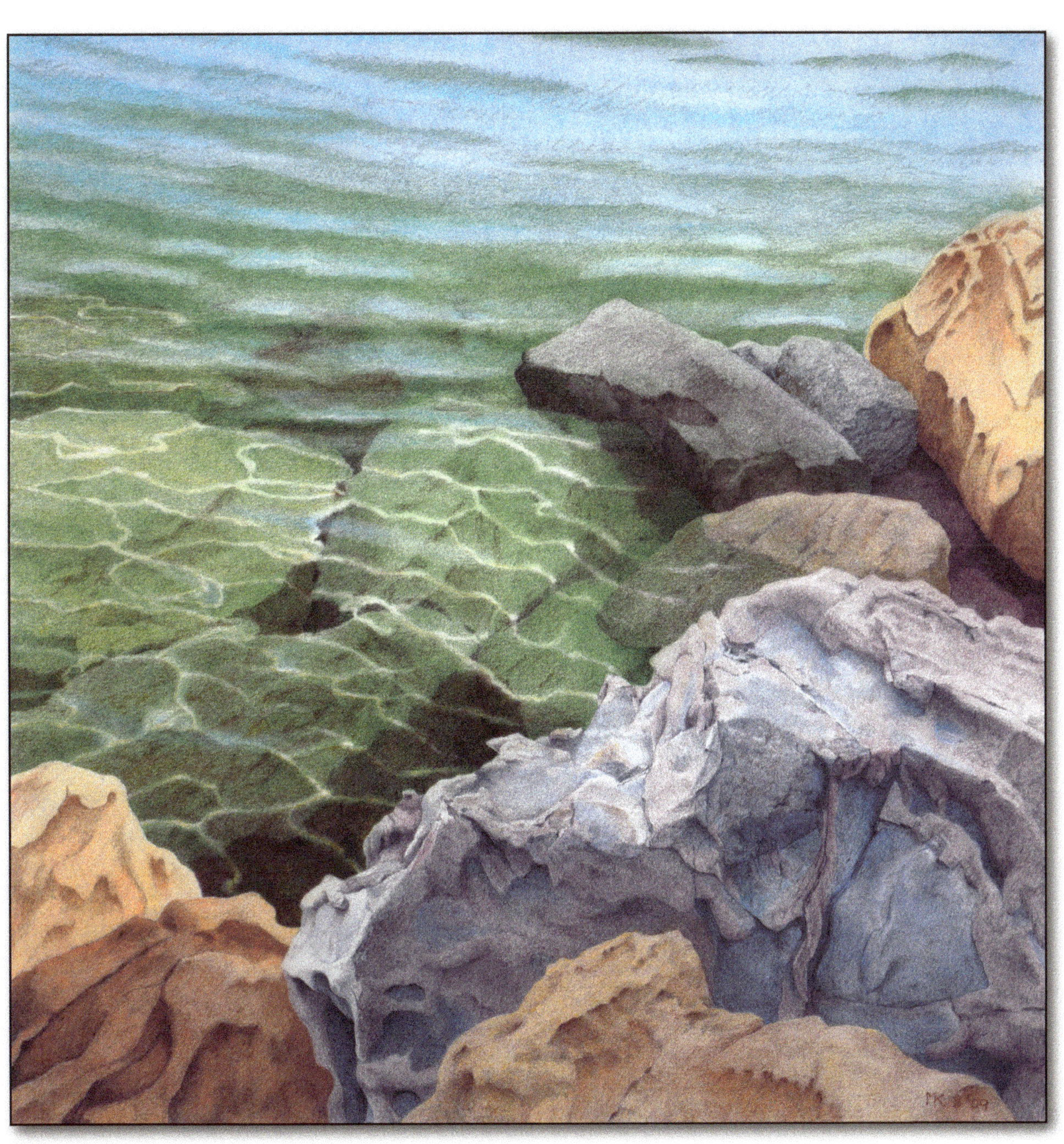

Rippling Water - 18" x 19"

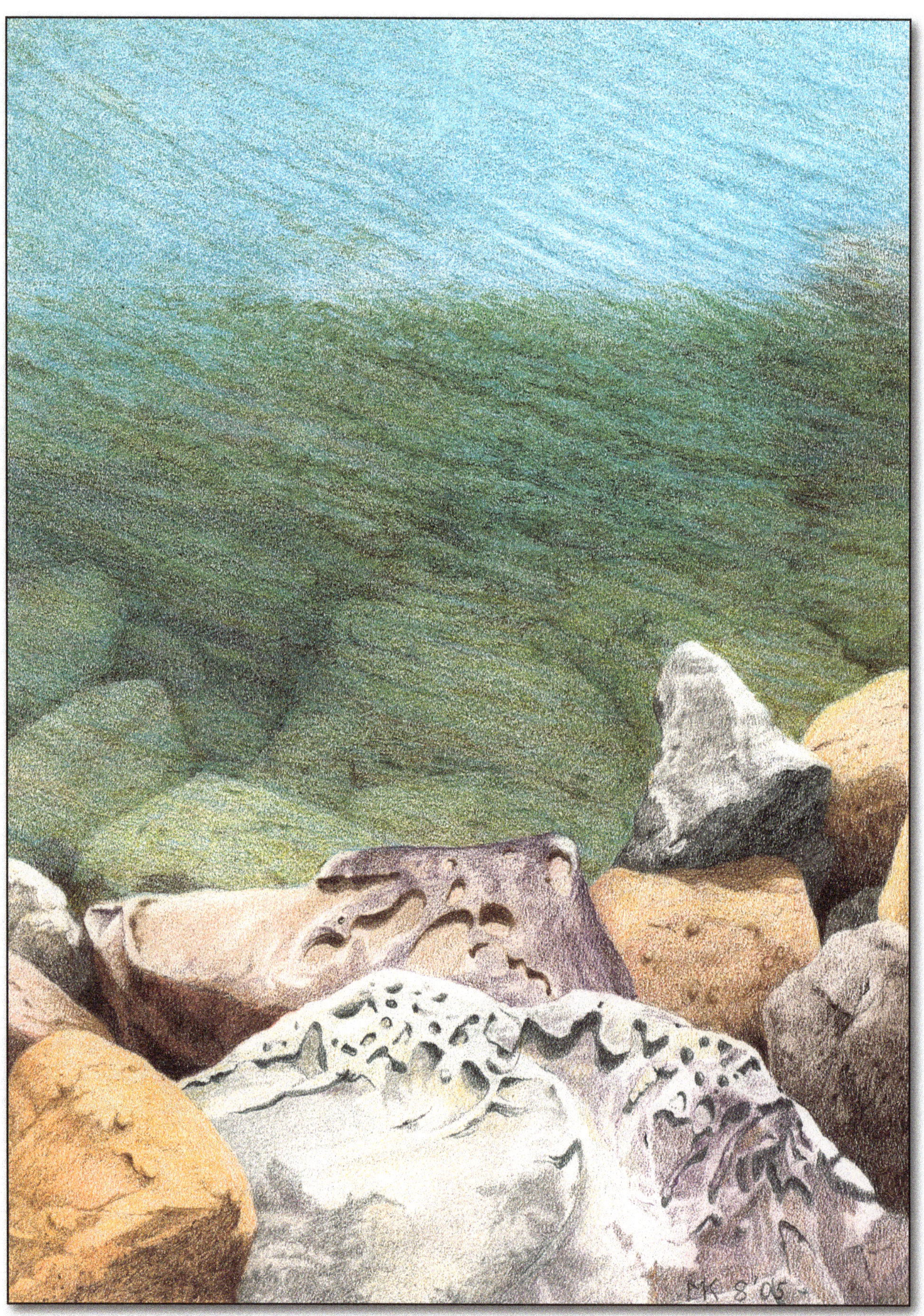

MK 8'05

About The Channel Island Jetty

At first it seems that all is chaos.
No order to the arrangement of stone on stone,
Or pattern within stone.
Just a tumble of rocks.

And indeed it is a tumble.
But not without order:
    The order of curves and angles as stone piles on stone.
    The order of gravity pressing stone to stone.
    The order of highlights and shadow as the sun sweeps over the sky.
    The order of earth colors - subtle grays, browns, ochers and rusts.
    The order of erosion changing each stone - layer-by-layer, particle by particle,
    creating beautiful shapes and lacy bar reliefs.

They've been dumped willy-nilly
to create a safe harbor against tides and storms,
moorings for boats, and as a way in and out of the deep ocean.
We may notice them in passing.

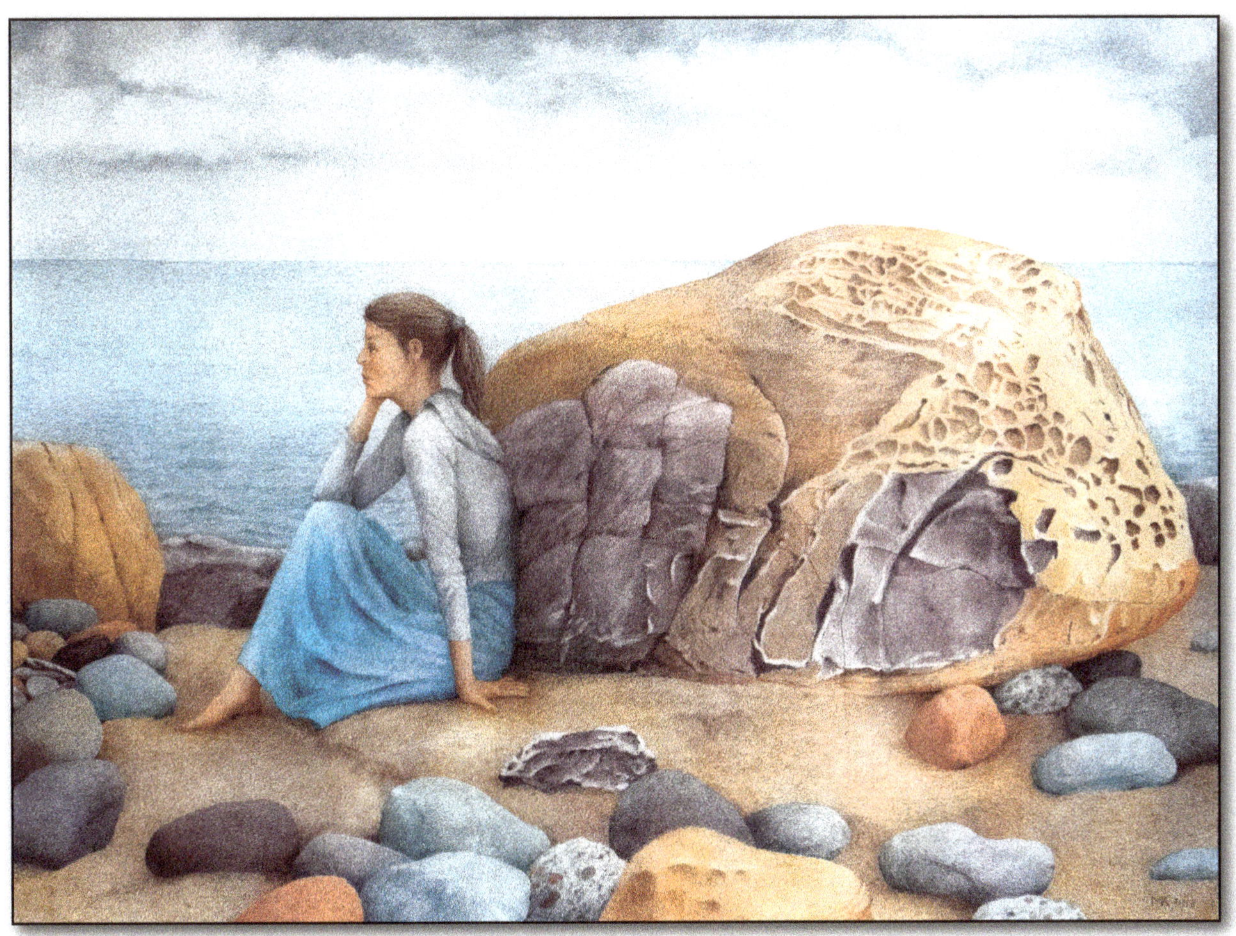

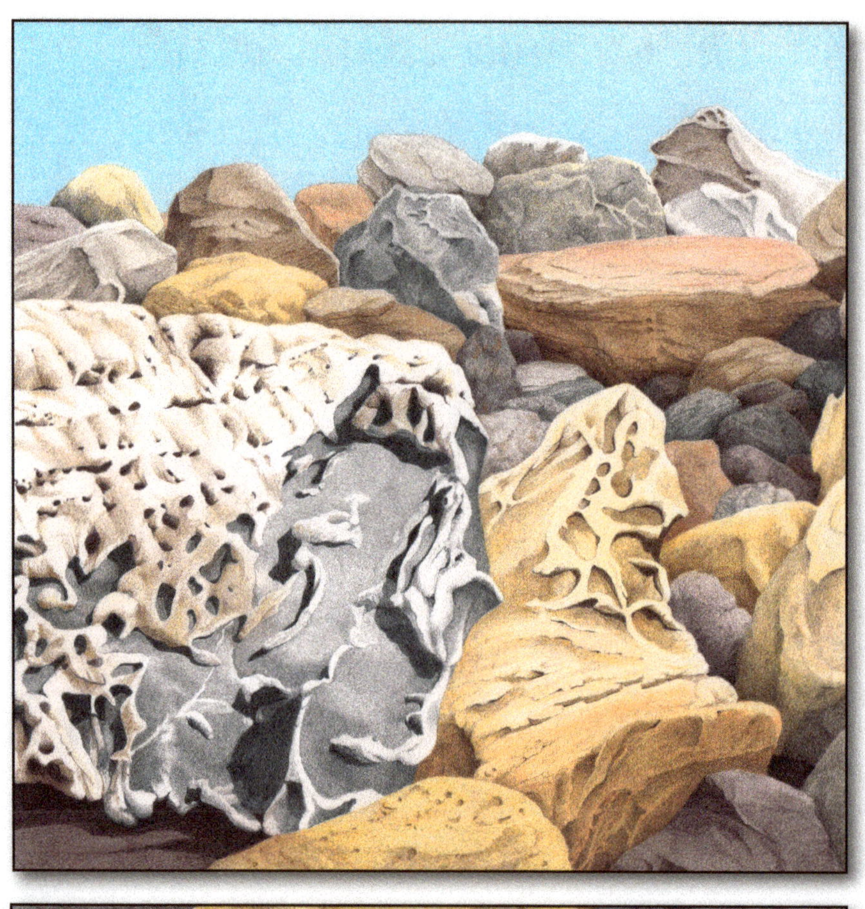
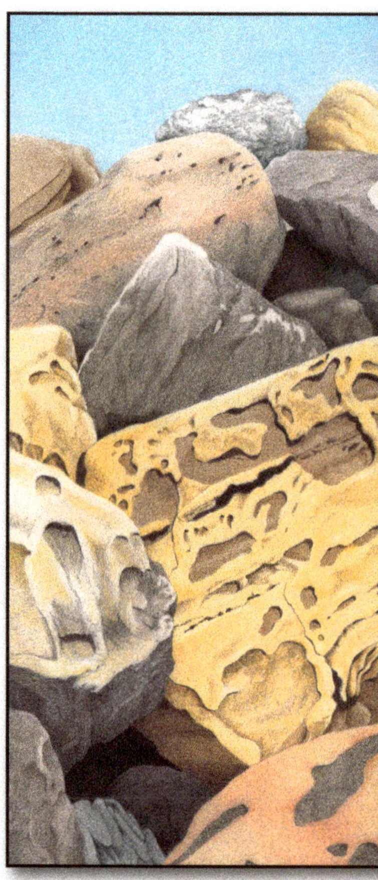
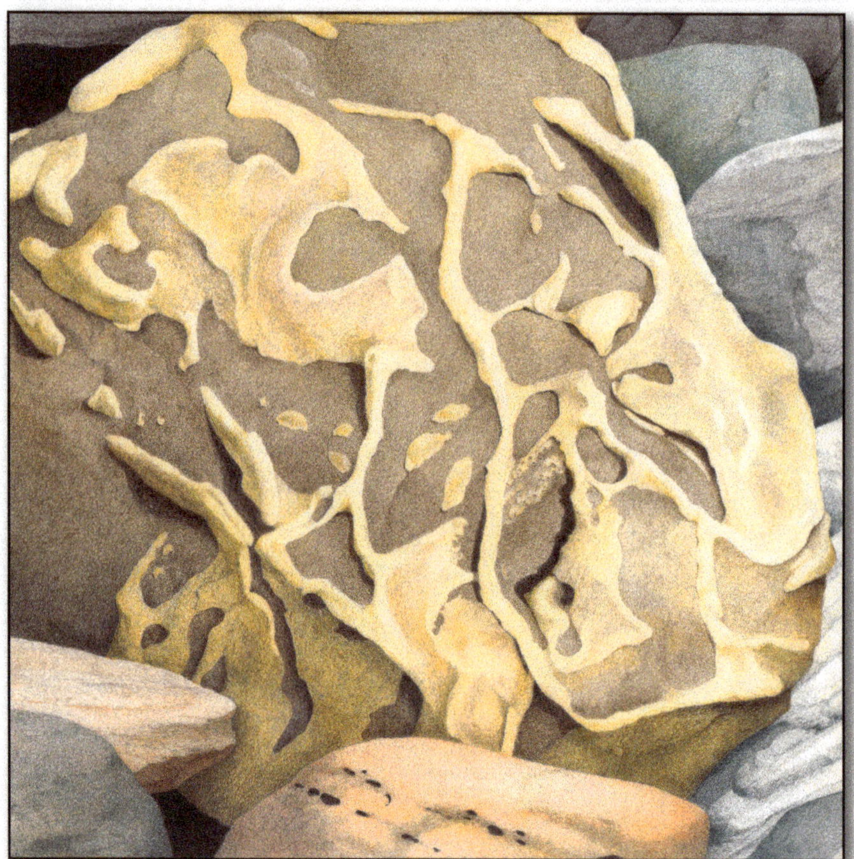
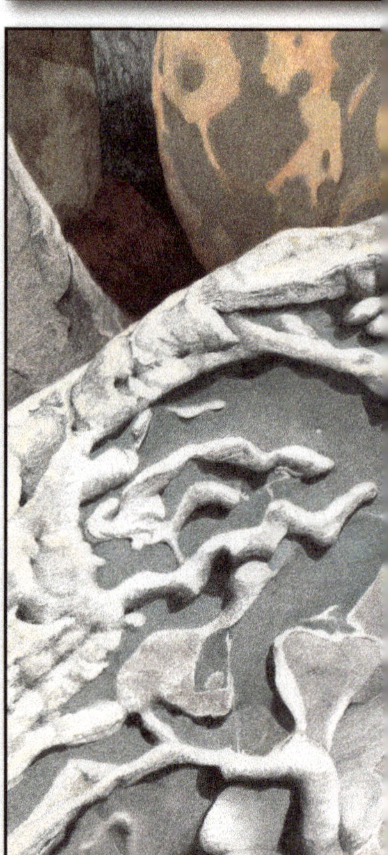

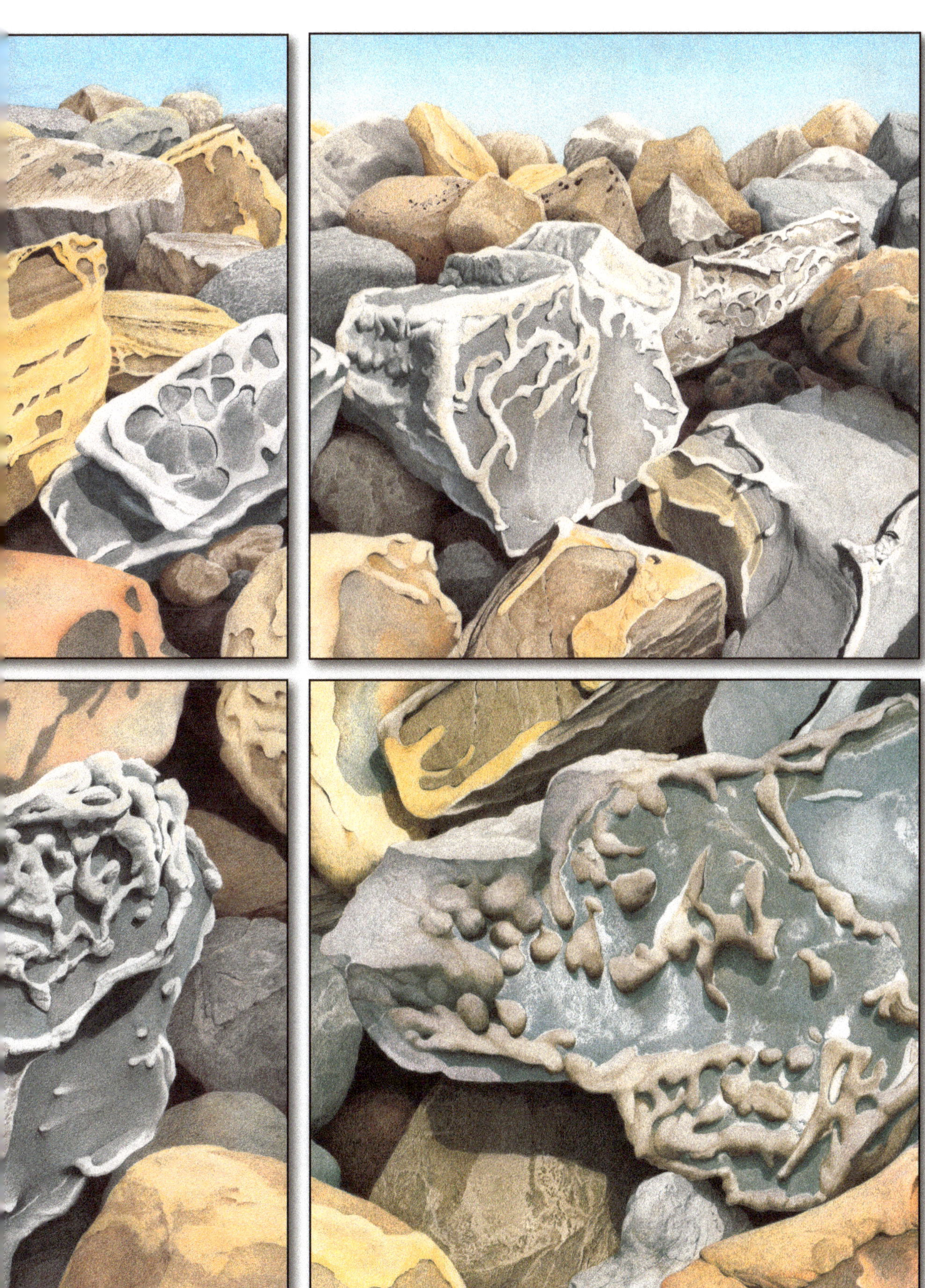

Rocks On The Jetty - 6 panels, 14" x 14"

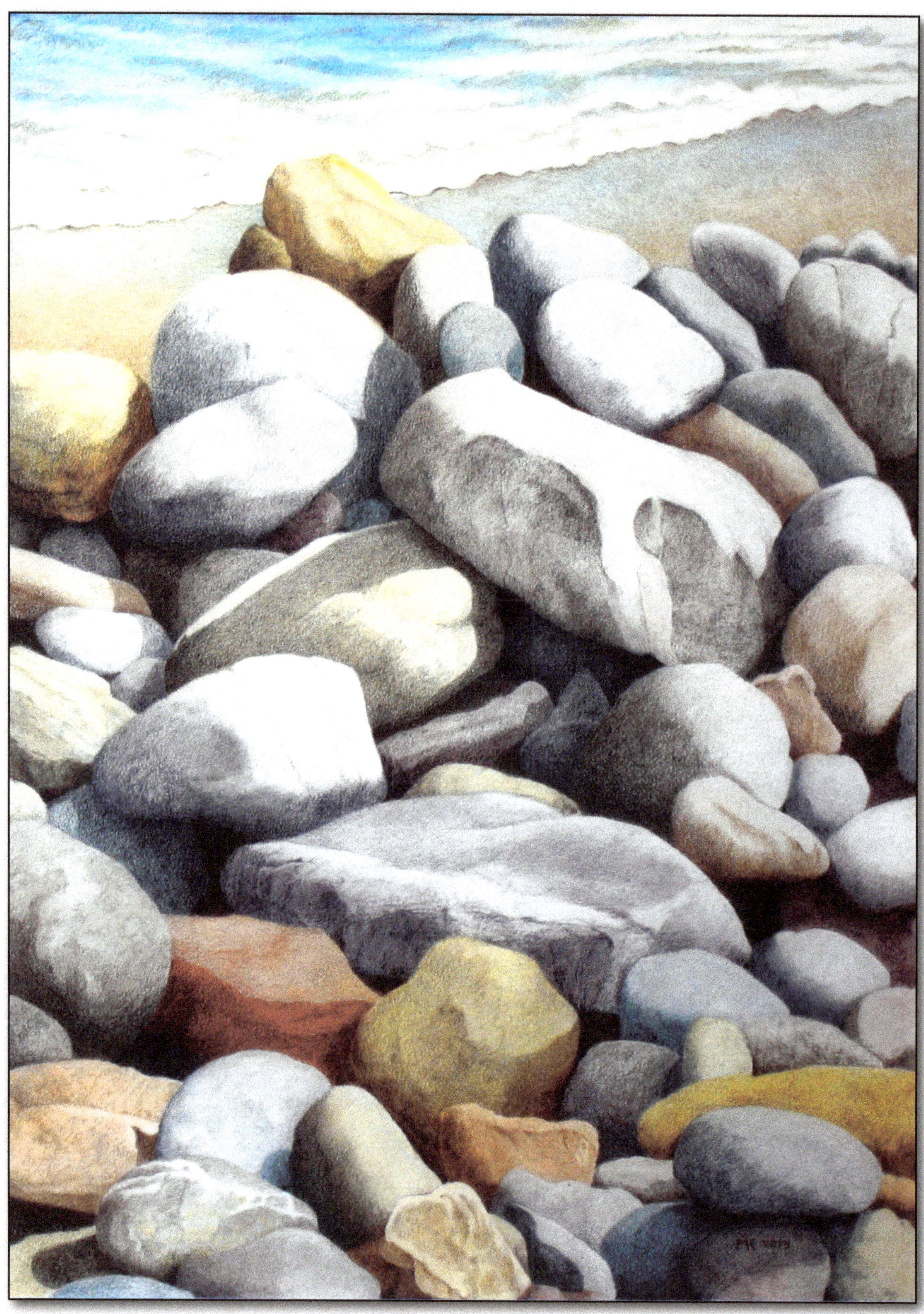

One Point In Time

I come from a dance background,
So for me, the rocks have dance qualities;
gesture, direction, flow,
physical dynamics such as leaning, pressing,
falling, resting, balancing.

As I draw them I ask;
     How does the water flow?
     How do the shadows move across them?
     How does one rock press against another?
I am choreographing a strange dance
of creation, erosion, change.

Ever new.
My drawing capturing
one Point In Time.

The jetty's rocks look like they'll last forever,
a permanent feature in the landscape.

Yet, even as I have been watching them,
these rocks have changed;

Mainly in small ways.
     A finger of sandstone, broken off,
     a wash of dusty chalk, blown clean,
     a line of one thin layer on another, deepened,
     a powdery coating, washed away.
The rocks dissolving into sand, become beach.

I can only show what I see now,
at this one point in time.

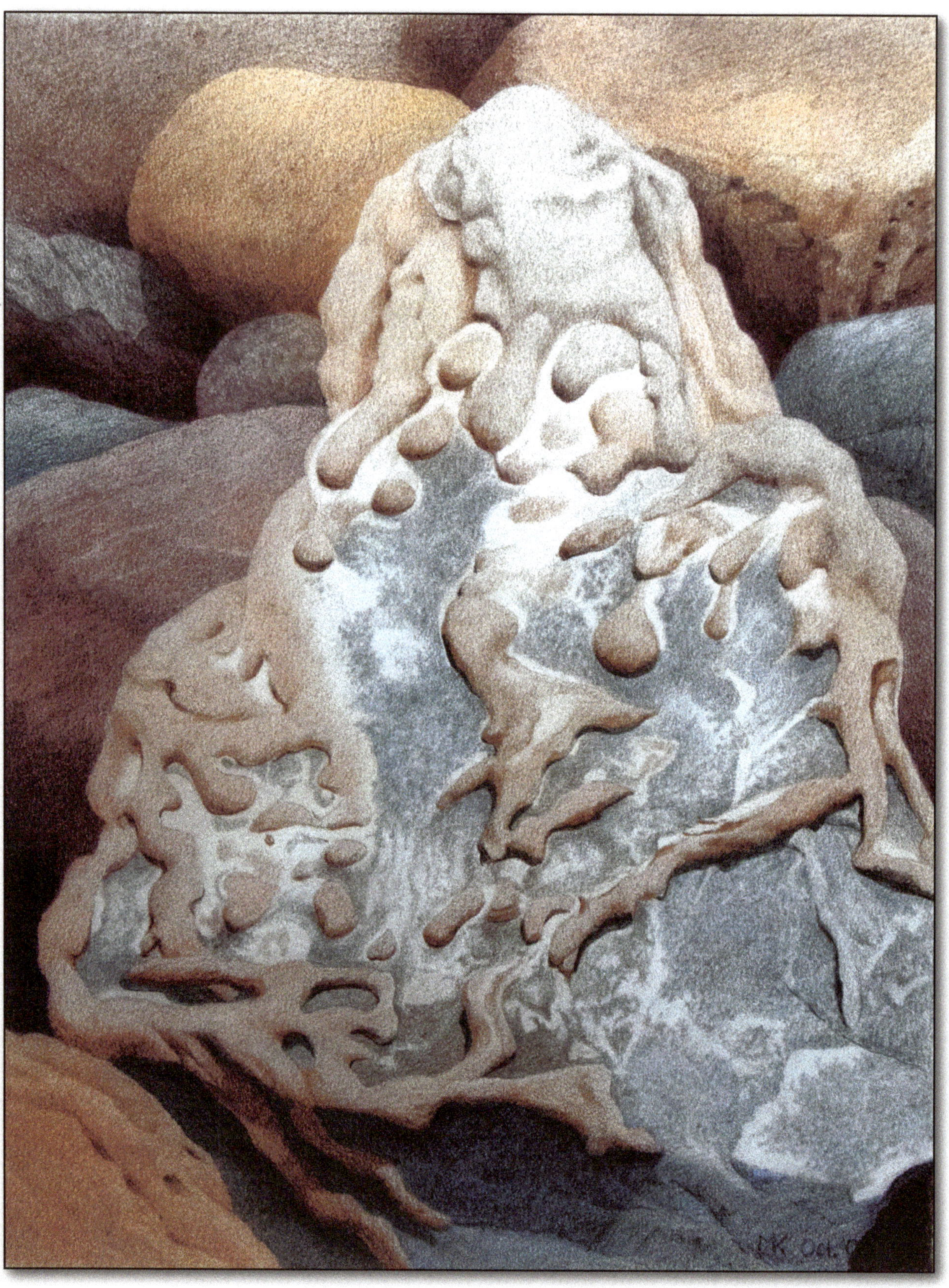

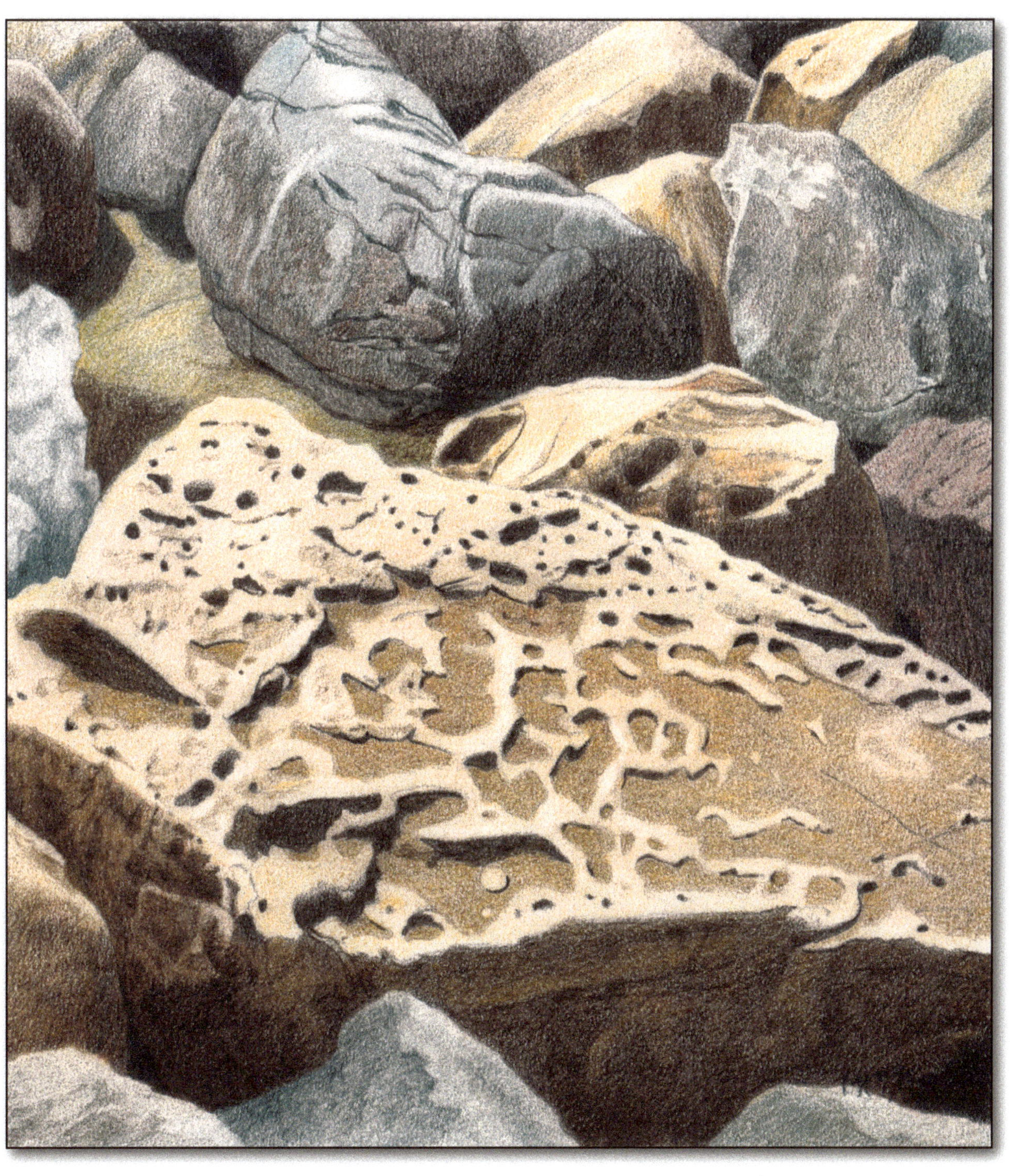

On Drawing Rocks

Rocks are bottom line. Everything else is built on them or of them. They are *star stuff* and remind us of our origins in the universe. Once they were all that was. Now, millions of years later, floating continents of hardened crust on a magma sea, they still define our lives.

I have always loved rocks. As a child I collected them, climbed on them, sat secure among them. As an adult I gather them as mementos of the places I have been. Their surprising shapes, their subtle colors and the eons of earth history that each individually represents moves me.

The rocks in these drawings were dumped willy-nilliy on the jetty at Channel Islands Harbor in Ventura County. Time and sea have sculpted them into extraordinary shapes. Drawing them has enabled me to become more aware of their strong and quiet beauty.

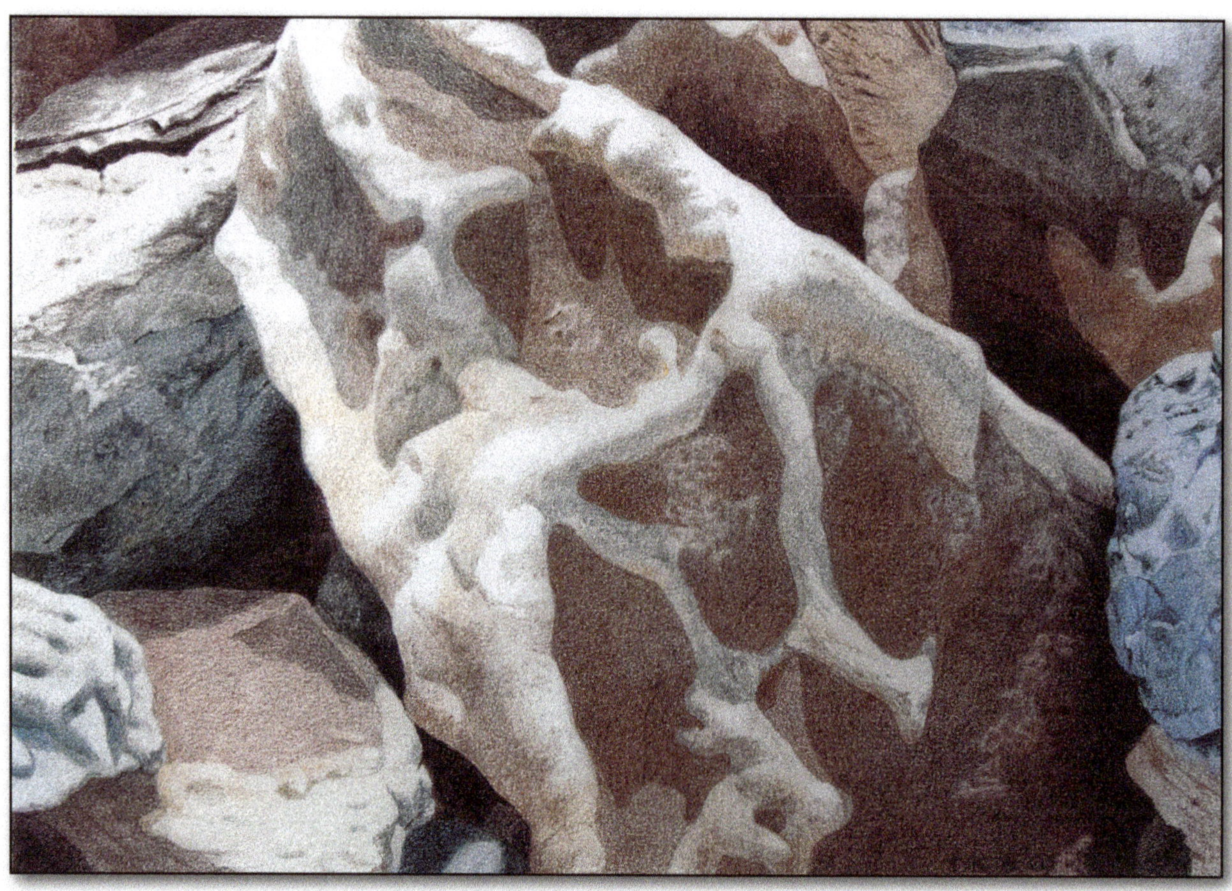

Erosions - 9" x 7.5"

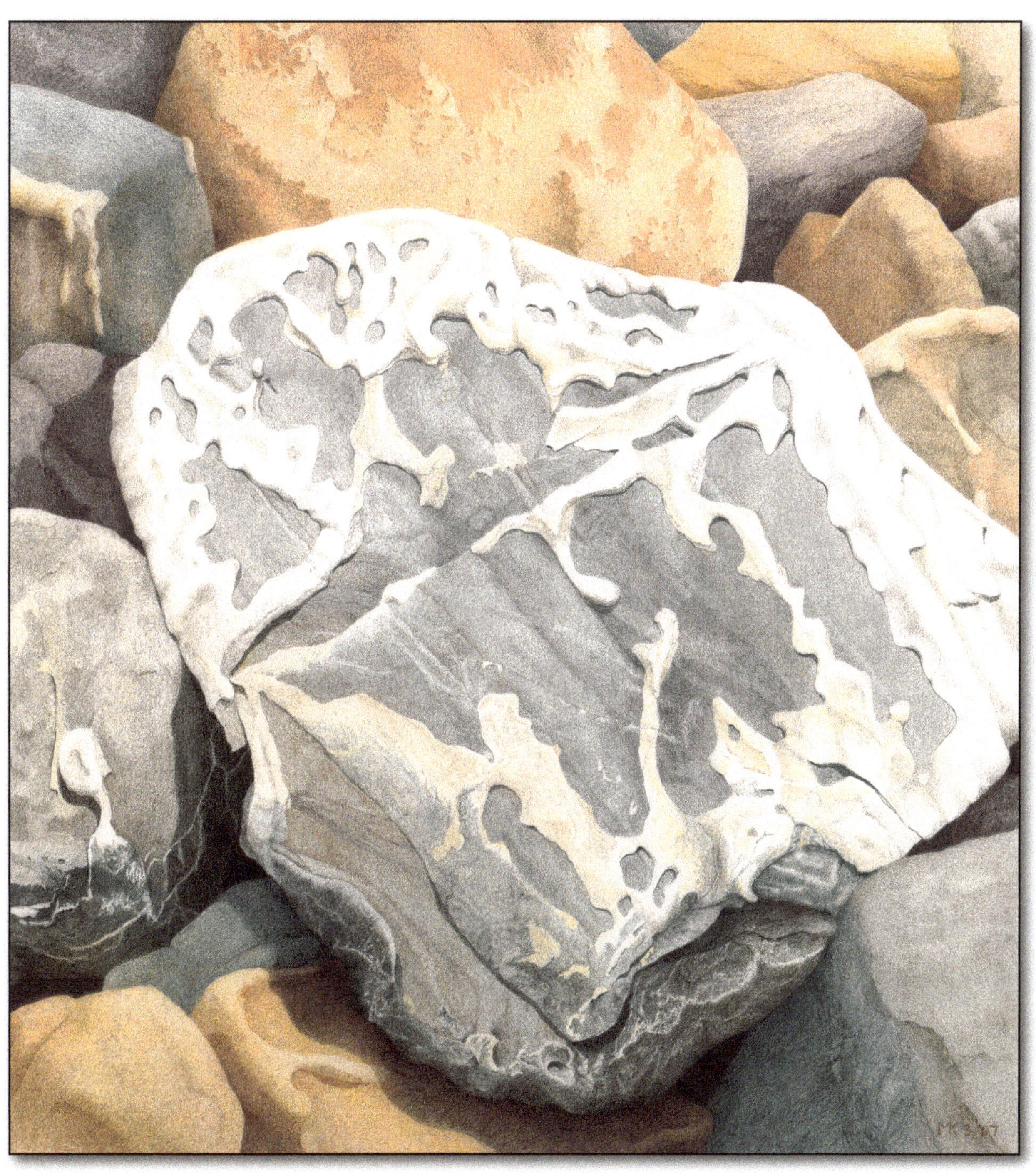

A Closer Look - 18" x 18"

I Love The Stories Rocks Tell:

Cataclysmic collisions of tectonic plates,
    The slow, irreversible pressure of vast oceans and lakes pressing down,
    everything, from giant skeletons to microscopic organisms, caught in the
    crush, volcanic eruptions - plasma from the core - bursting out,
    mountains quaking, tilting, breaking apart, their layers bending,
    wind and water, rain and flood eroding.
The planet in constant creation.

    Everlasting.
    Always changing.
    Becoming as they disintegrate.
    Evolving natural sculptures.
    Developed over eons.

When I draw rocks I enter into the timeless mystery of creation
and find my place in the universe.

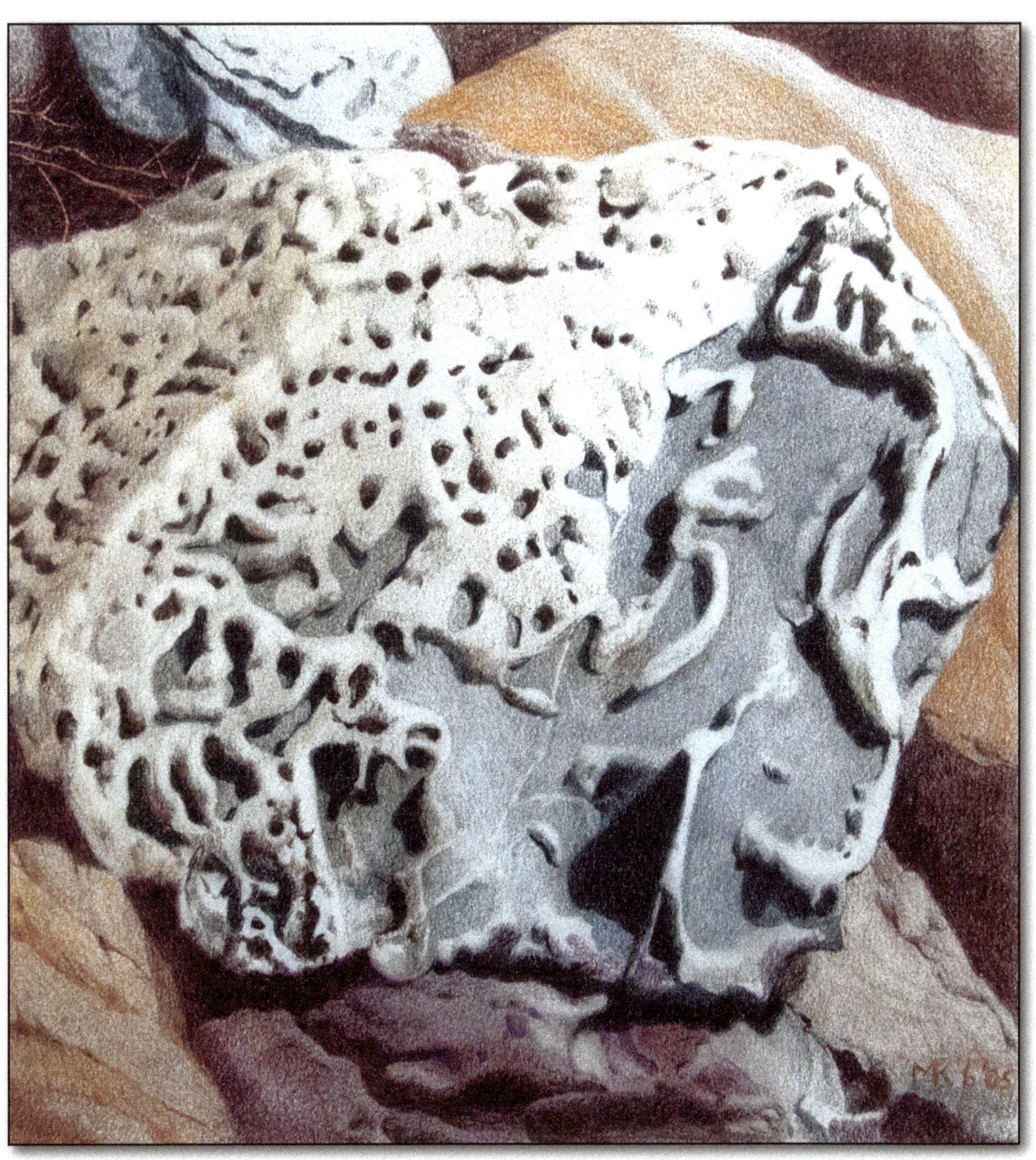

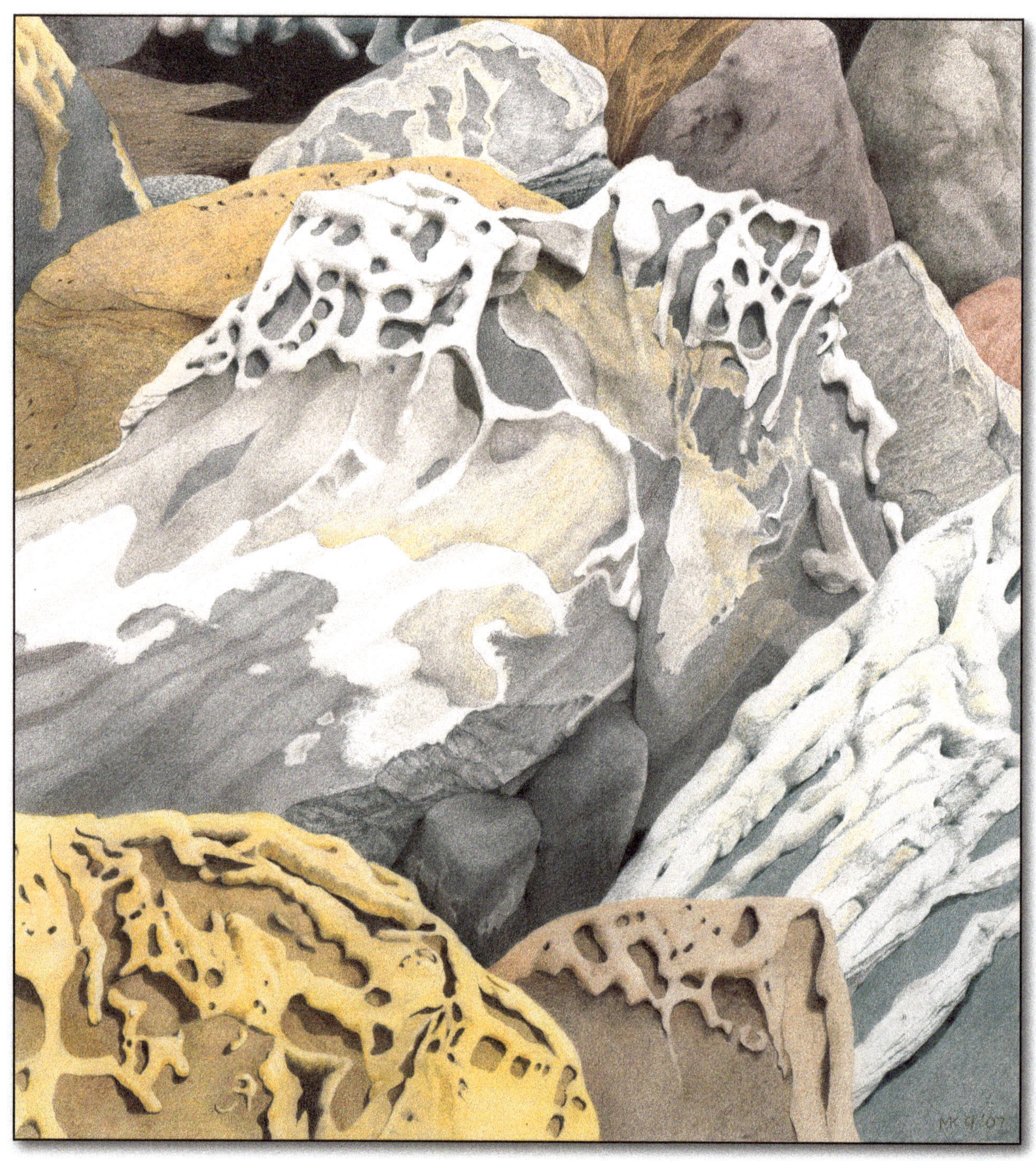

Erosion - 18" x 18"

Rock formations magnified

These drawings are as much about the water that carved and eroded the rocks as about the rocks, themselves. I was often guided by my sense of how water flowed across the rock surfaces. Magnifying the rock gave me an opportunity to focus even more on the subtle forms and beautiful grays and beiges that play against each other in these convoluted, fluid shapes.

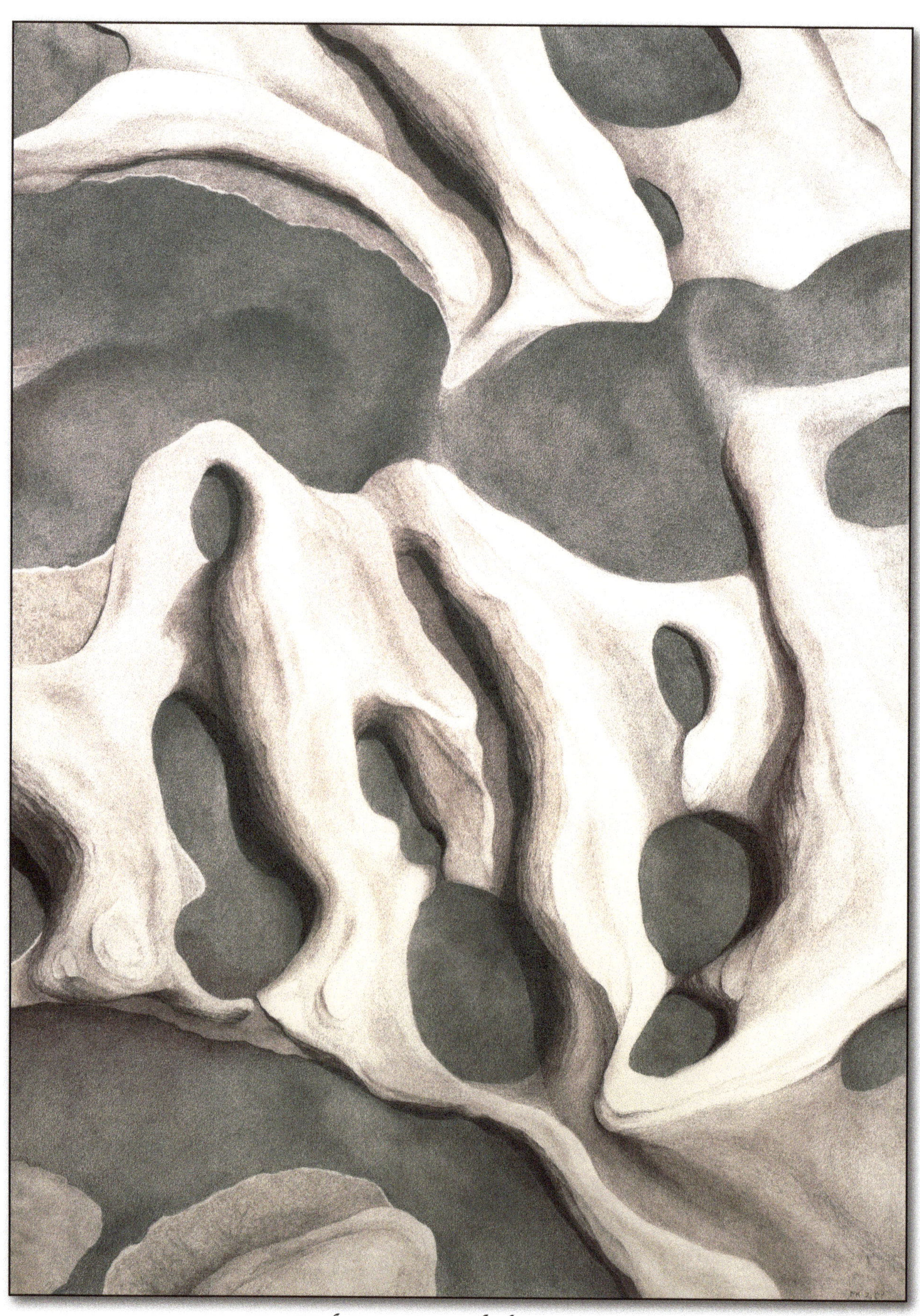

Rock Forms Magnified - 27" x 39"

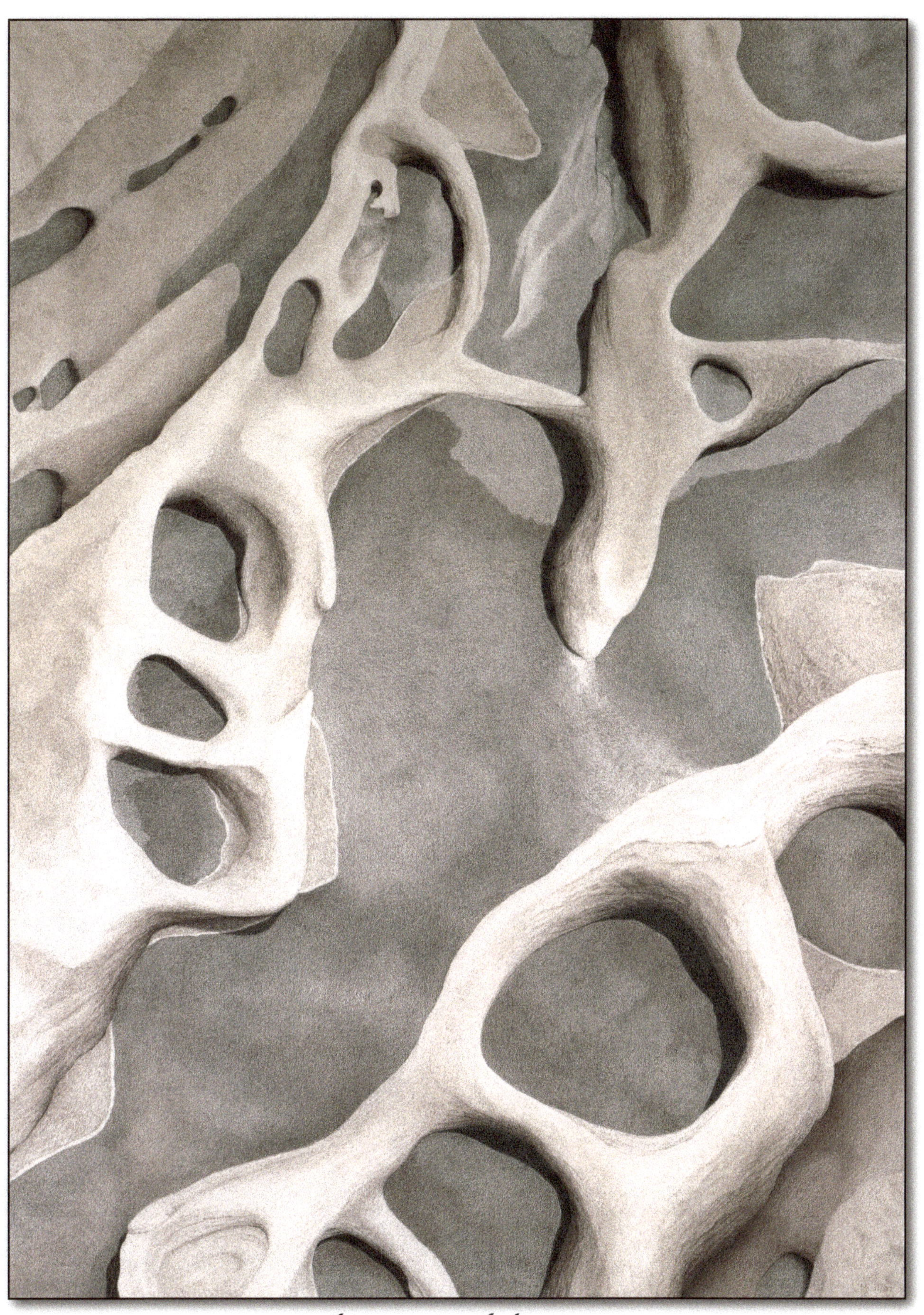

Rock Forms Magnified - 27" x 39"

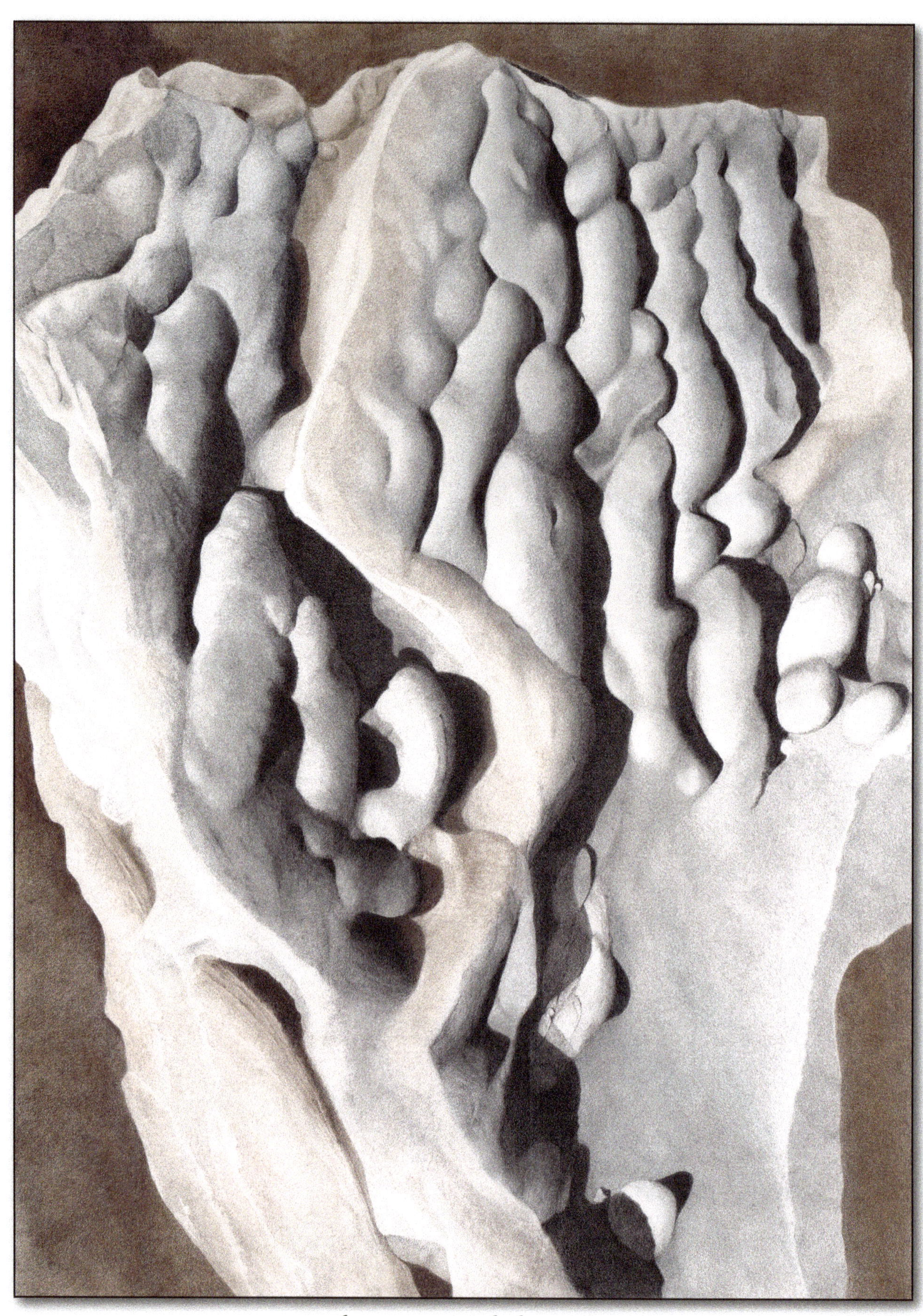

Rock Forms Magnified - 27" x 39"

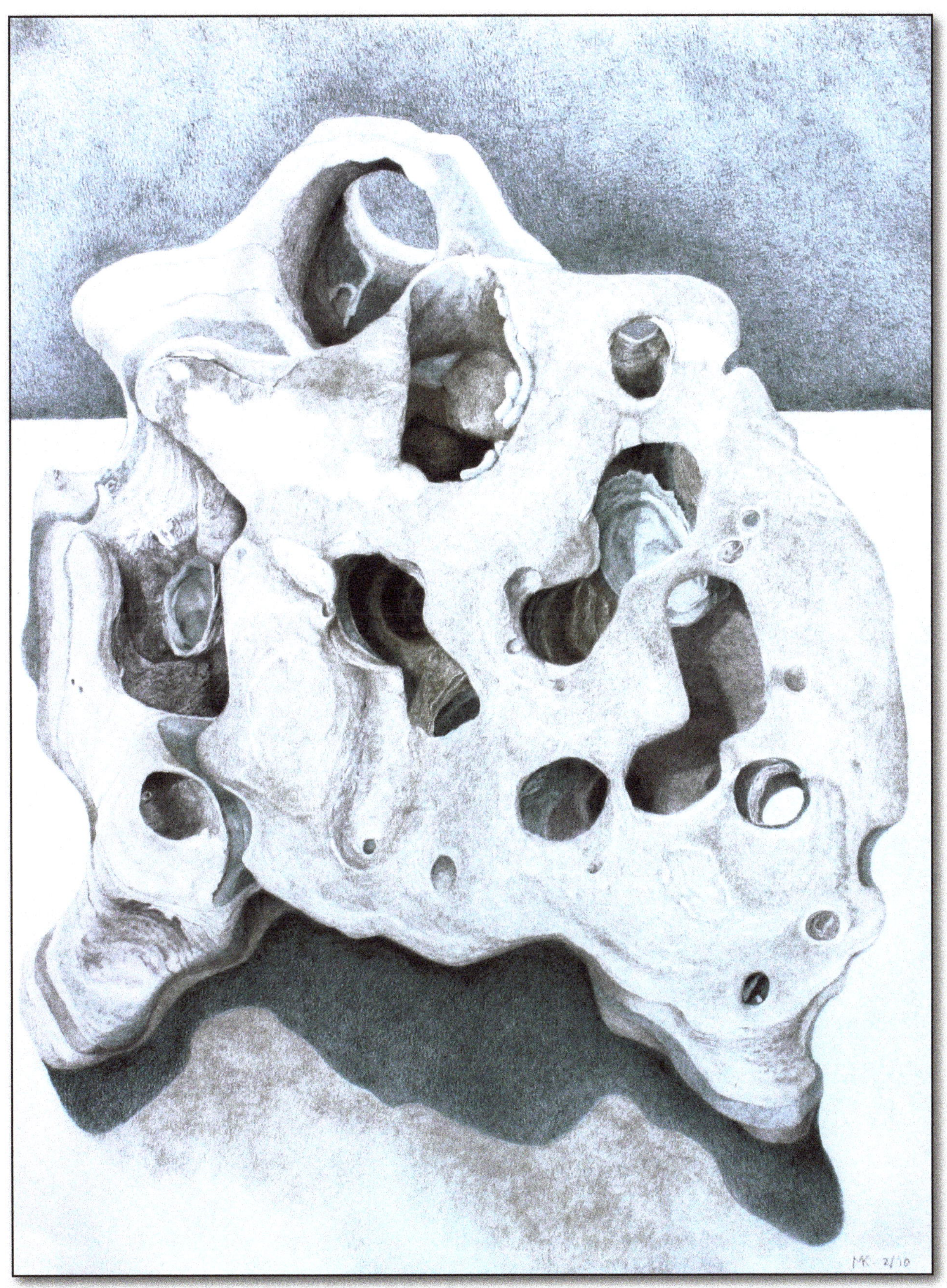

Sea Rock - 18.5" x 23"

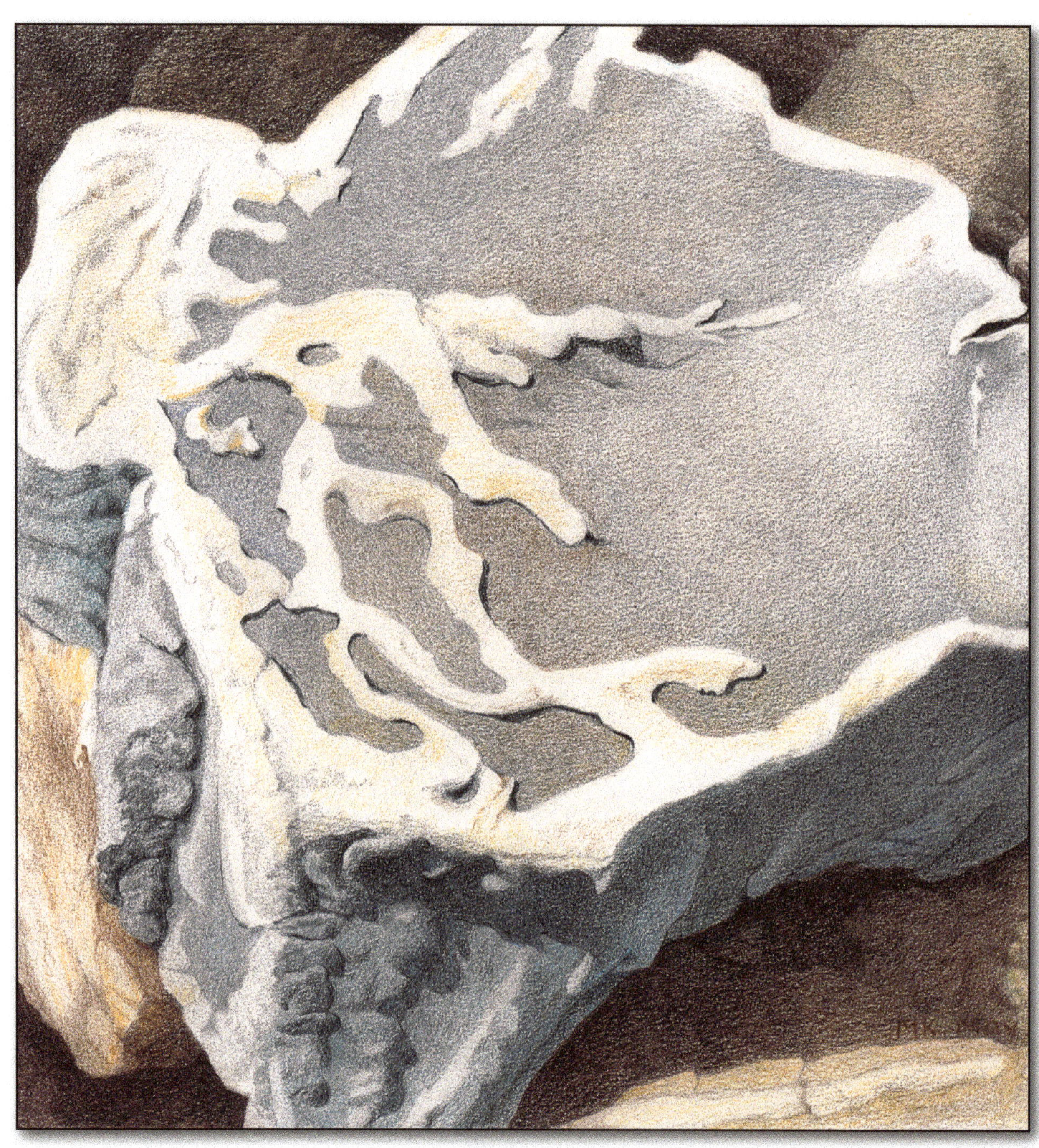

No Name - 7" x 9"

Part 3
Collecting Material

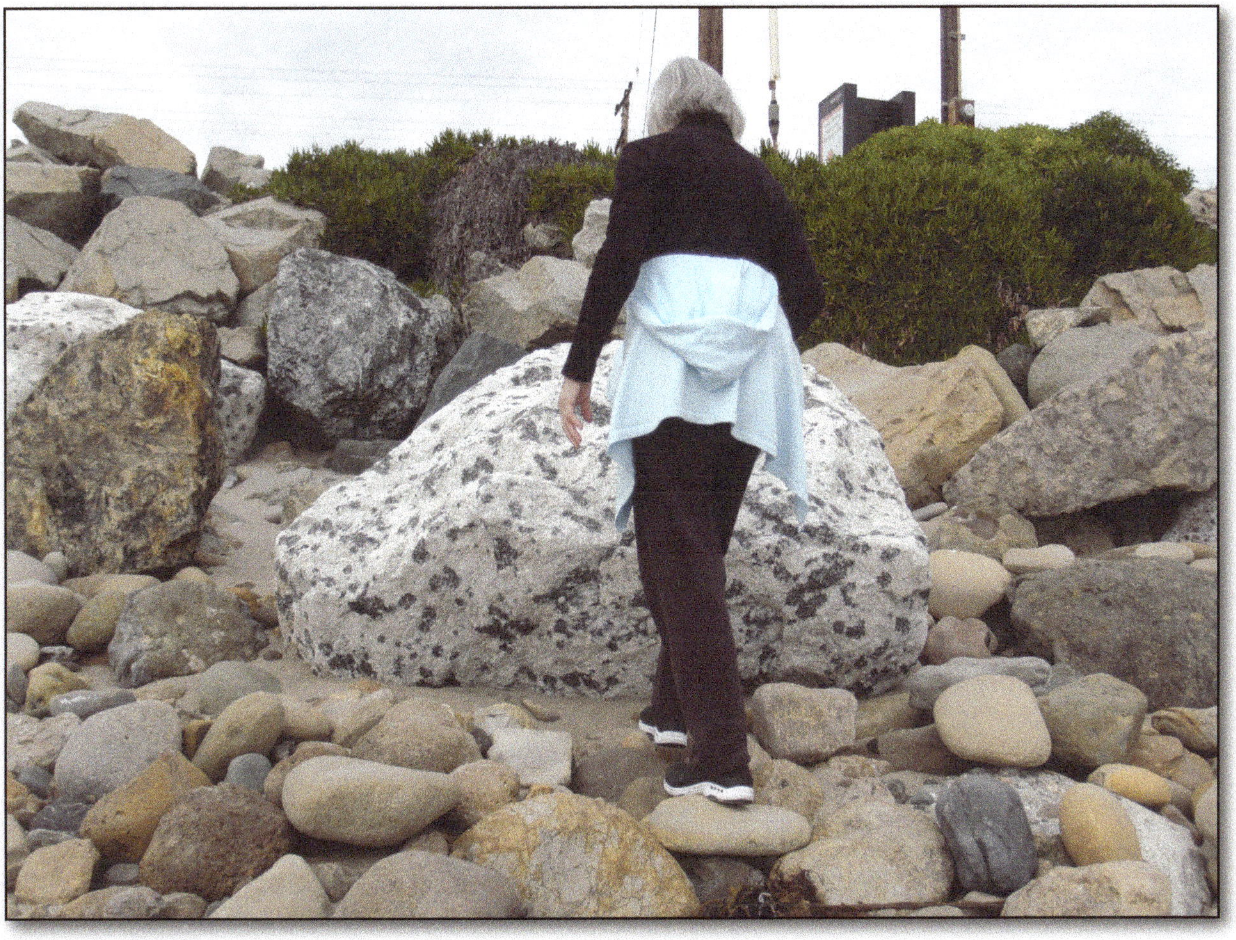

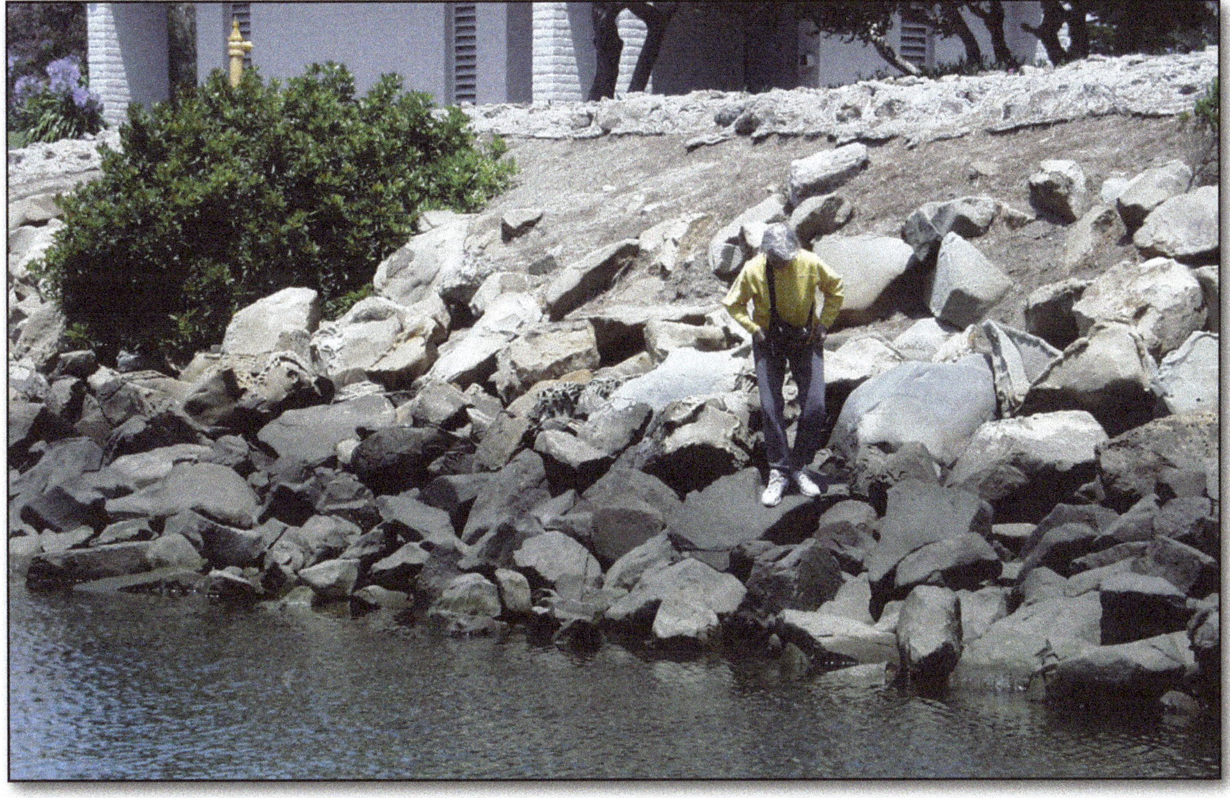

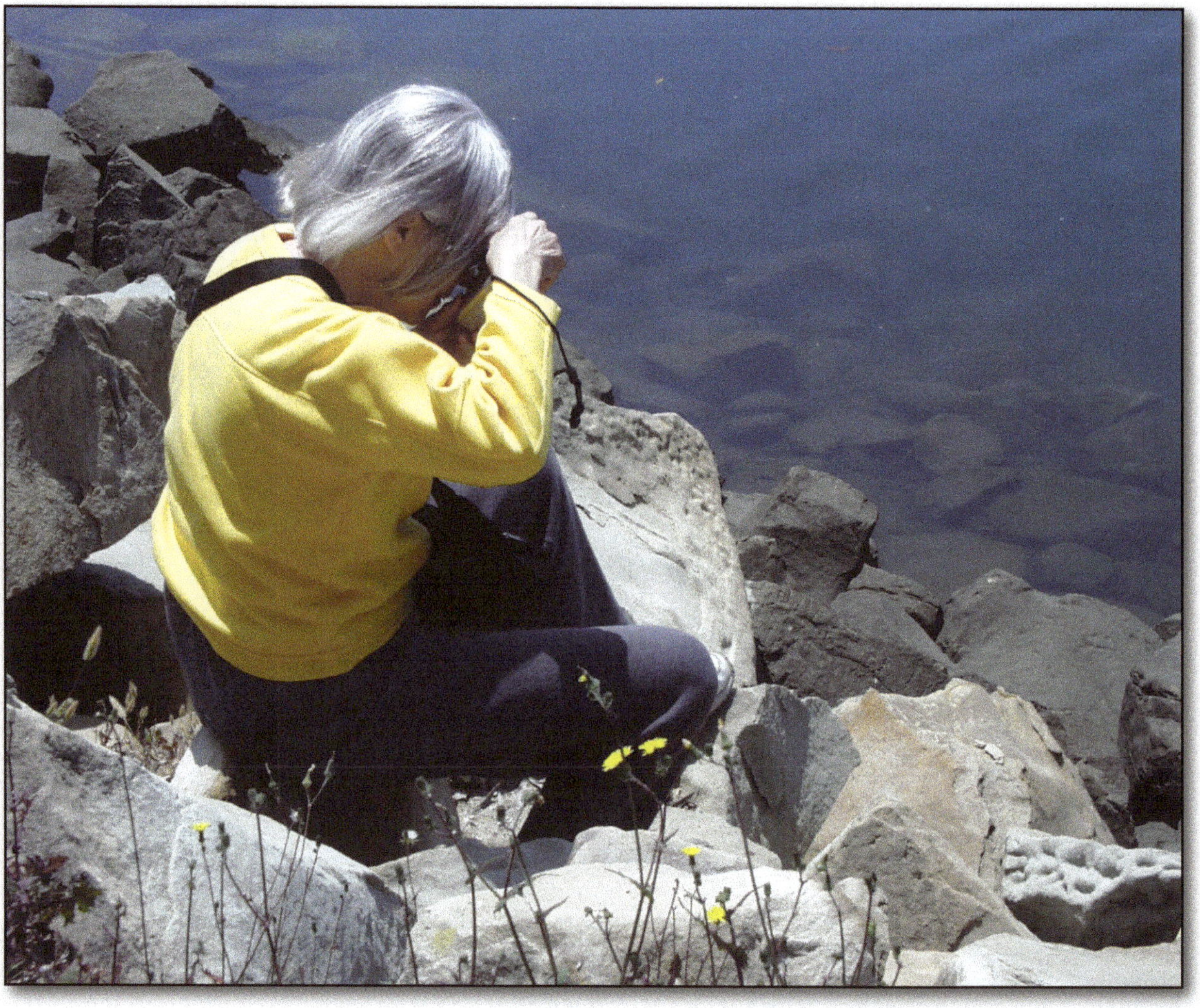

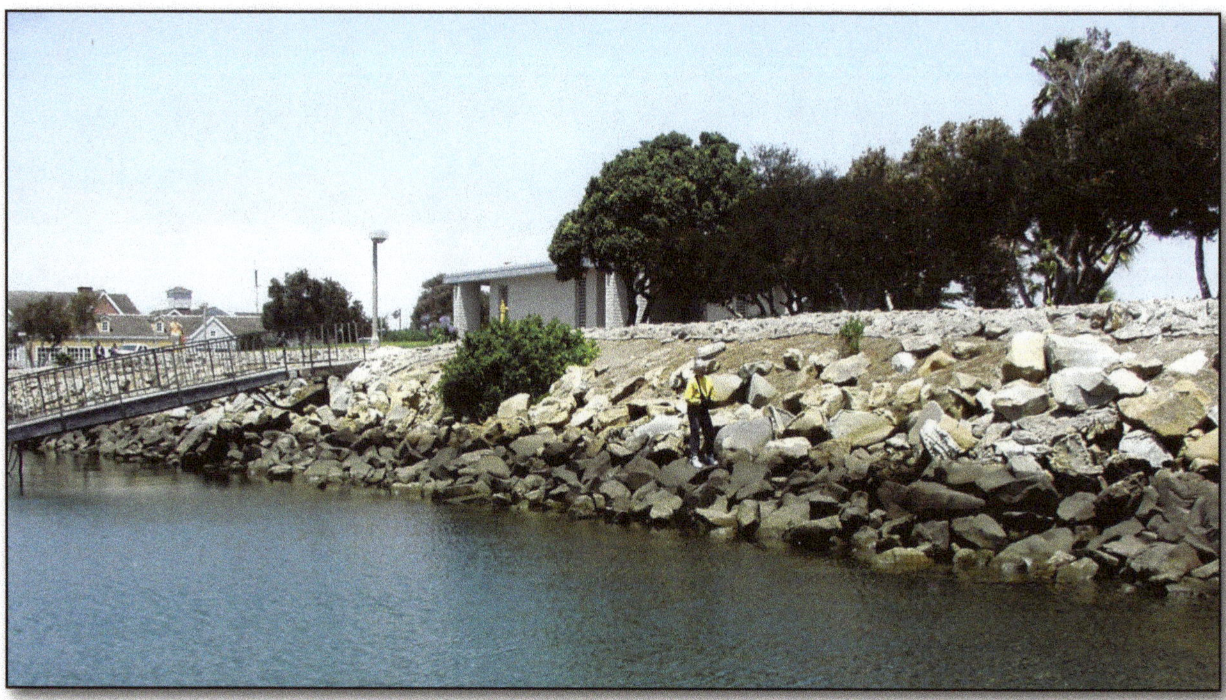

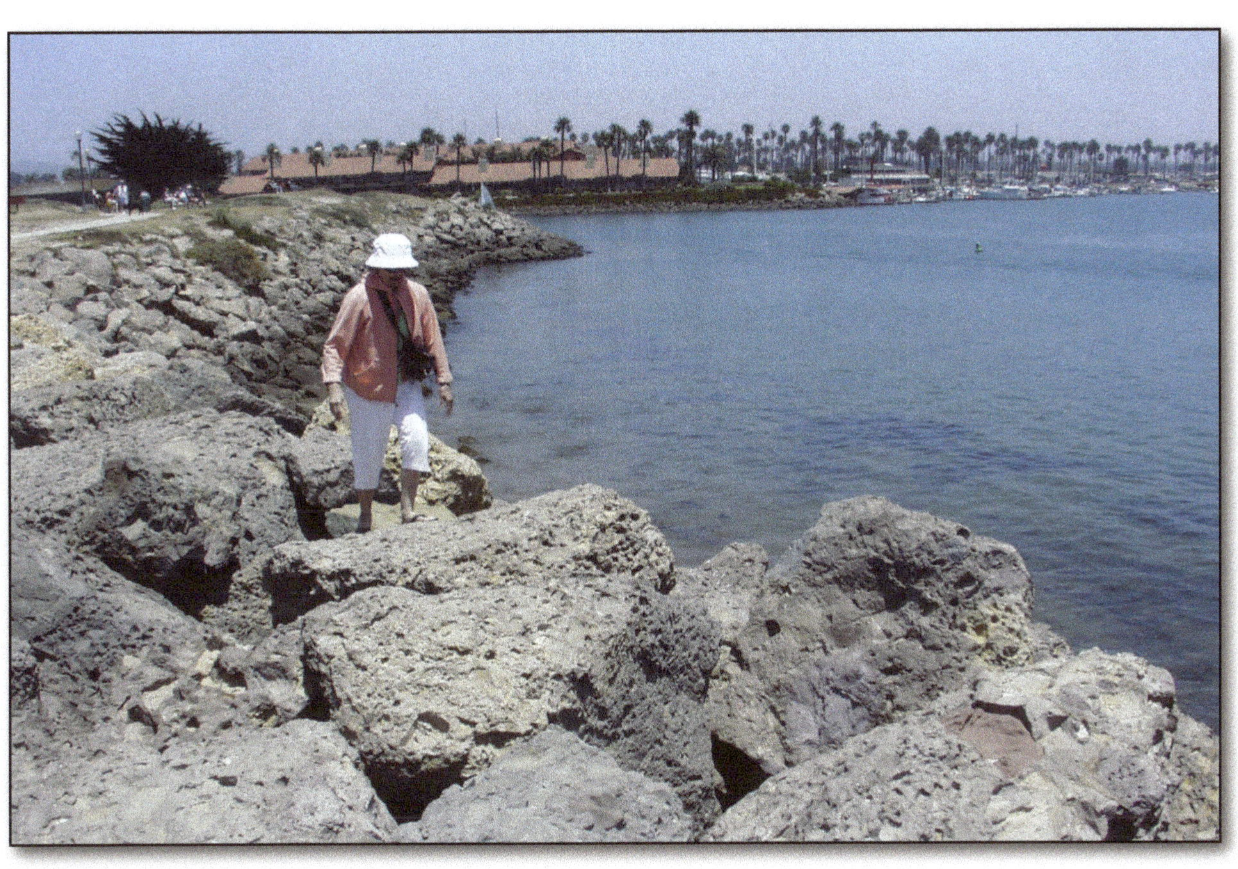

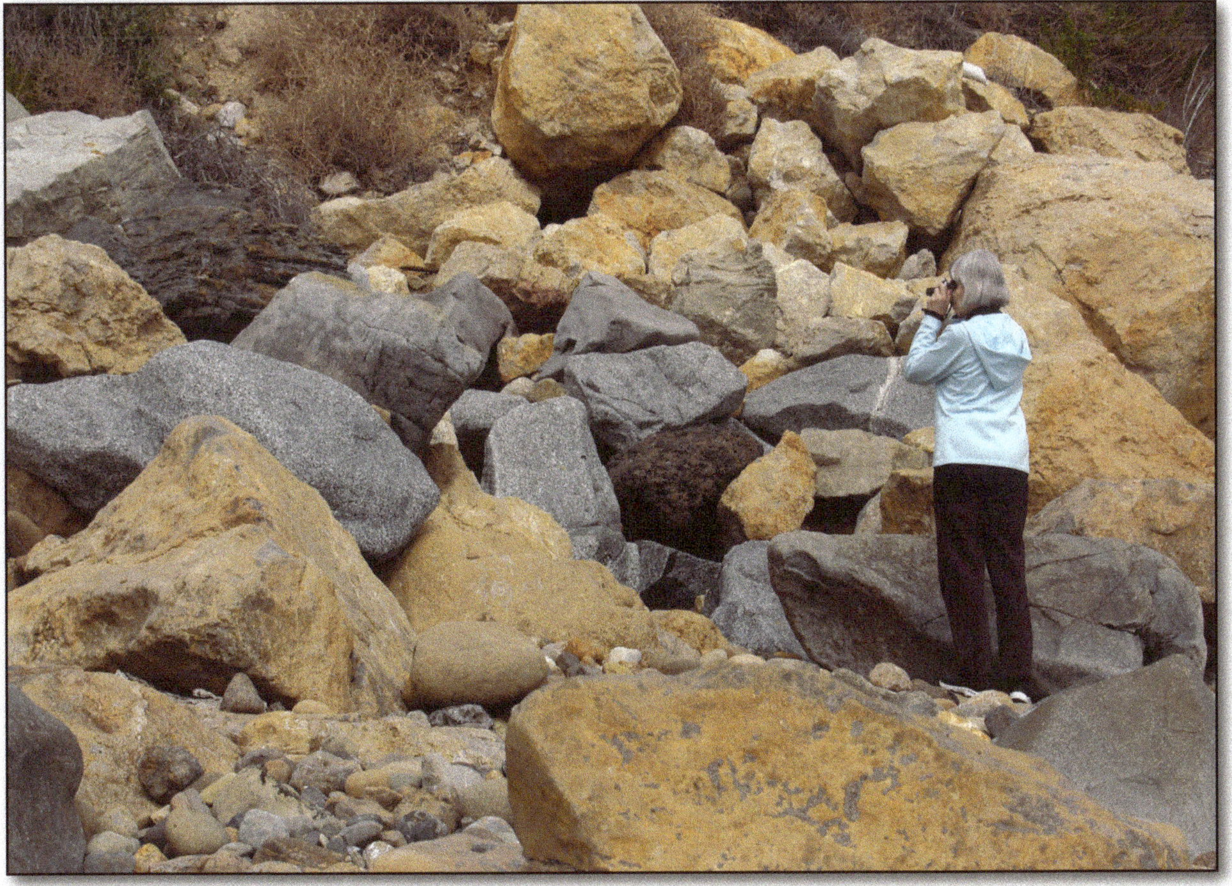

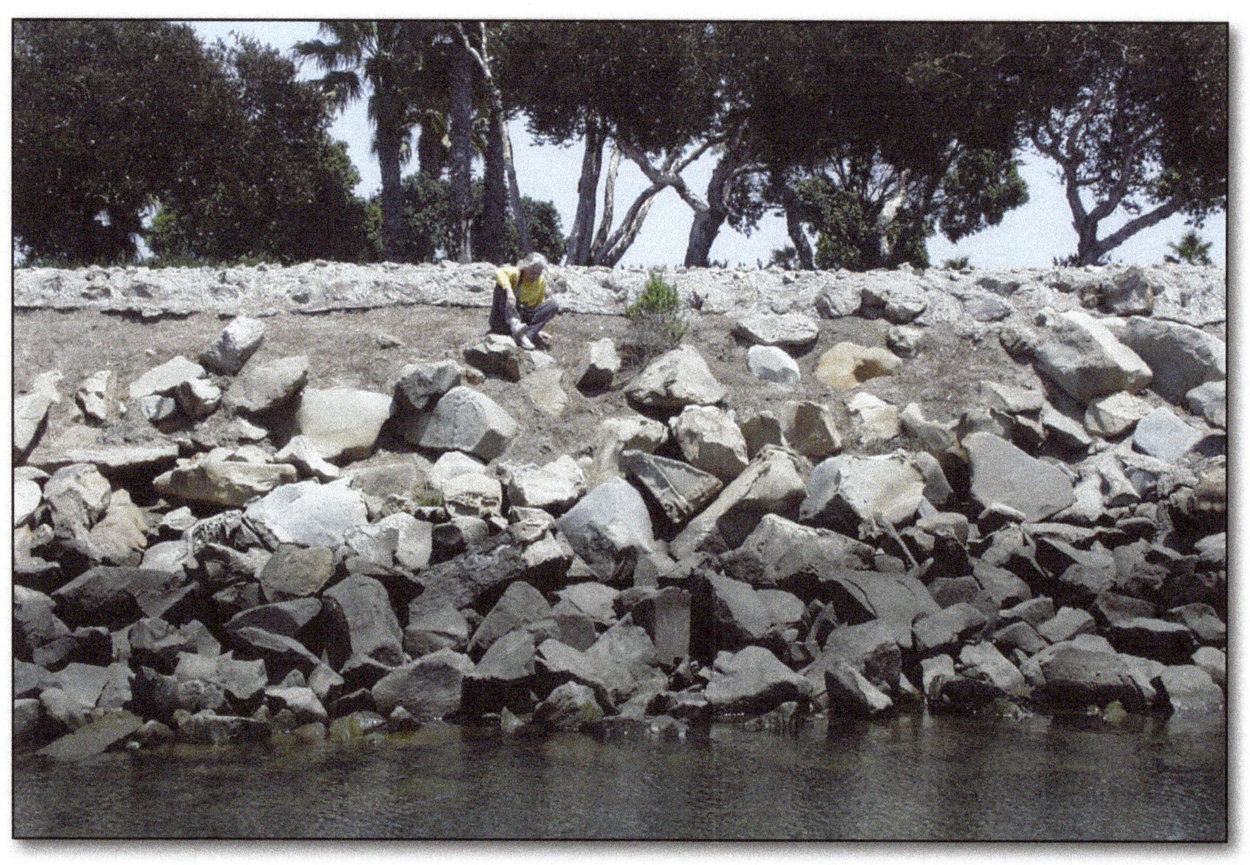

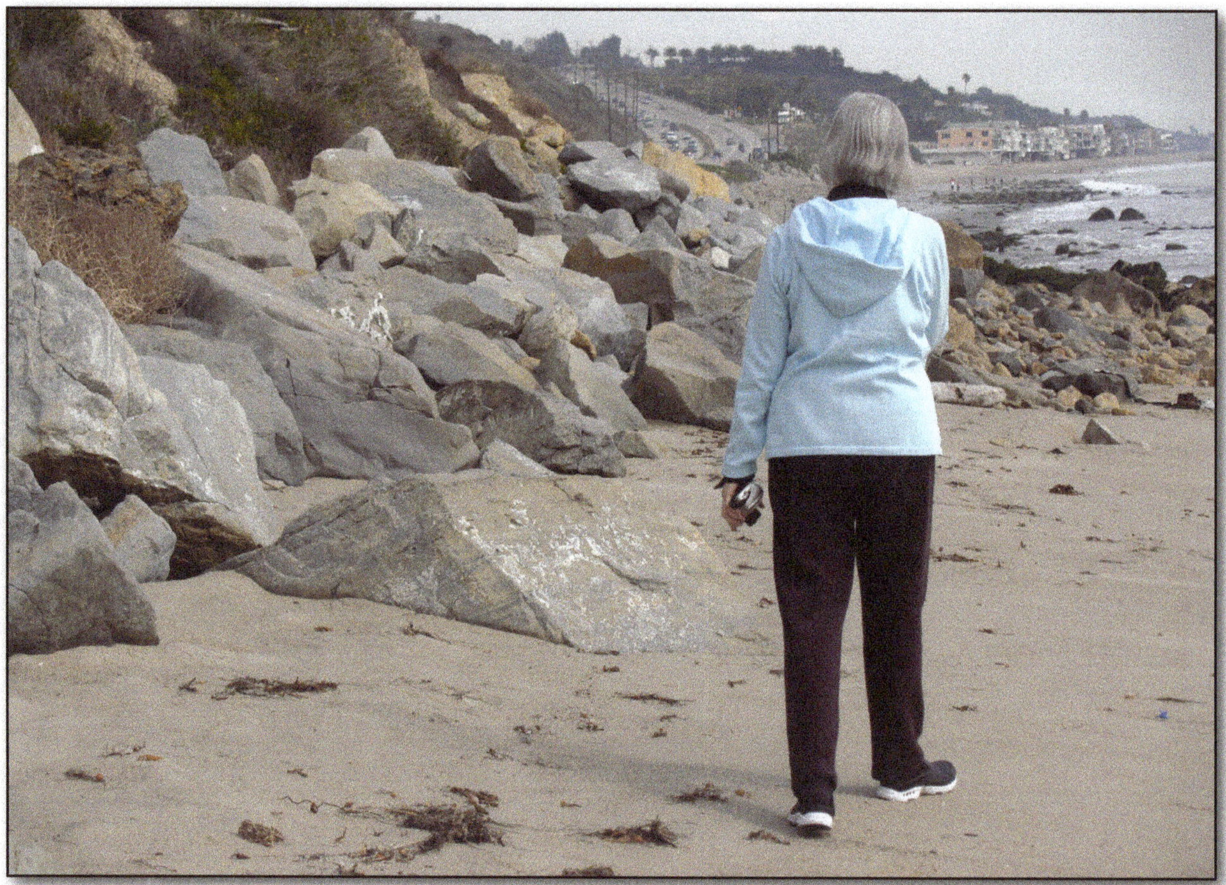

Part 4
Energy, Love, Humor

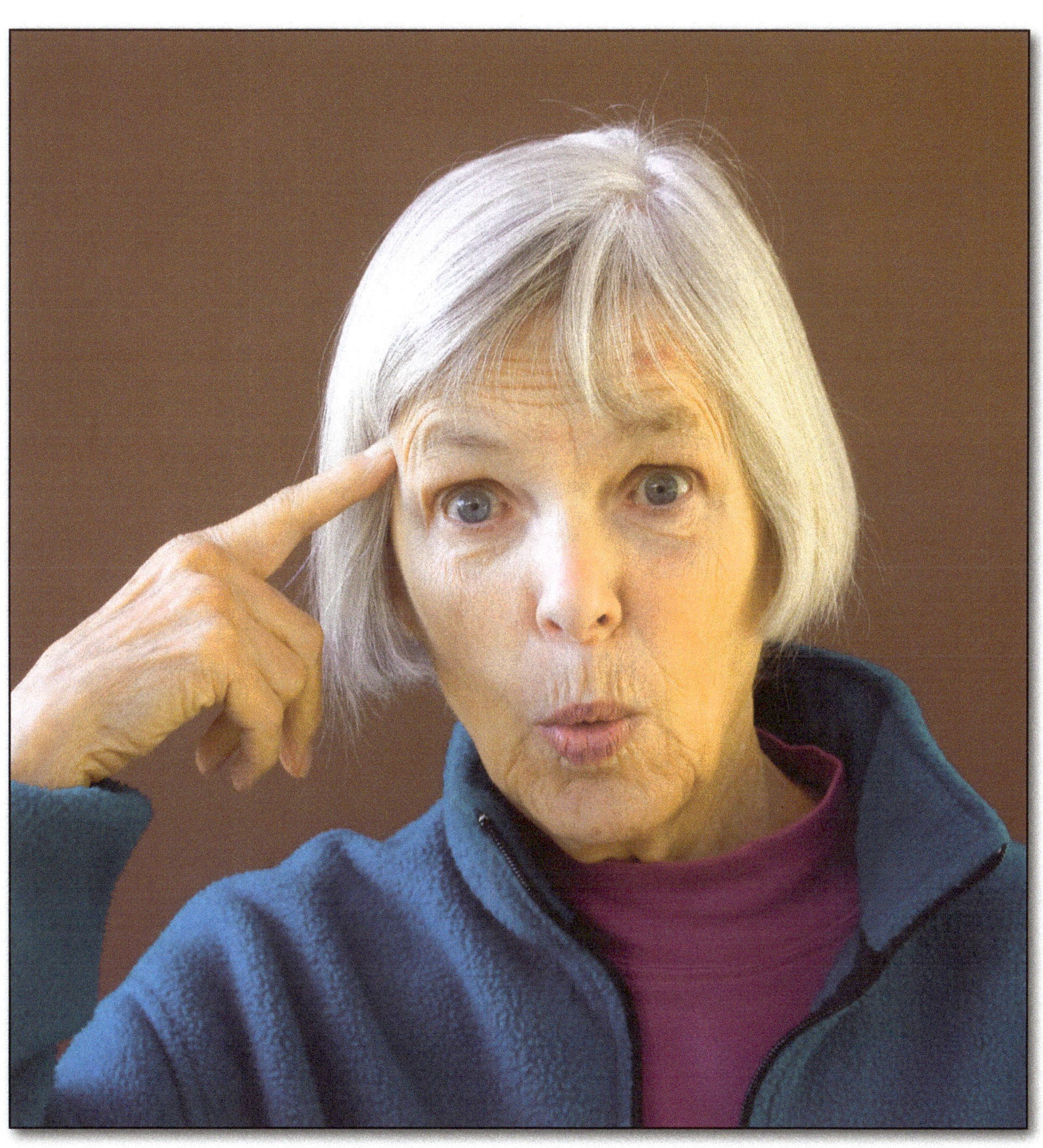

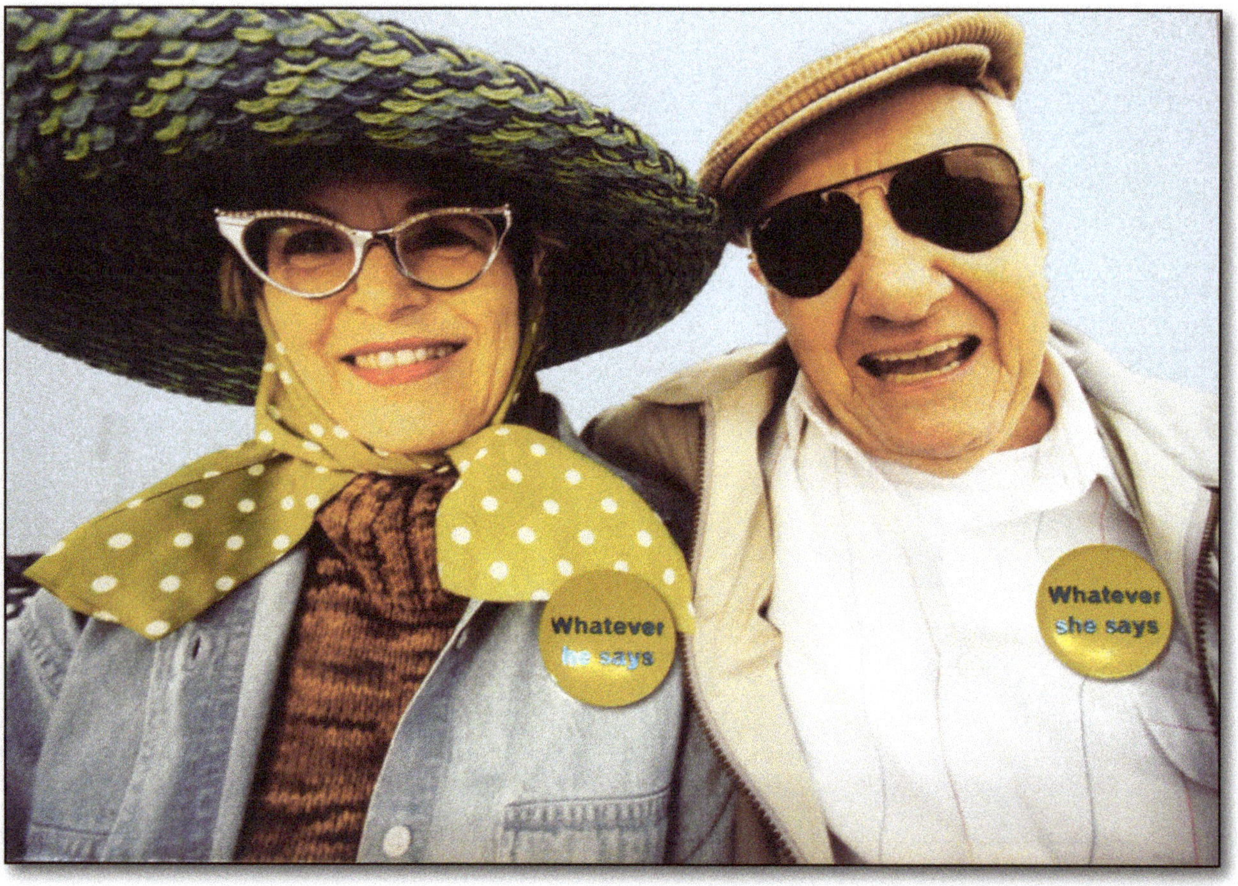

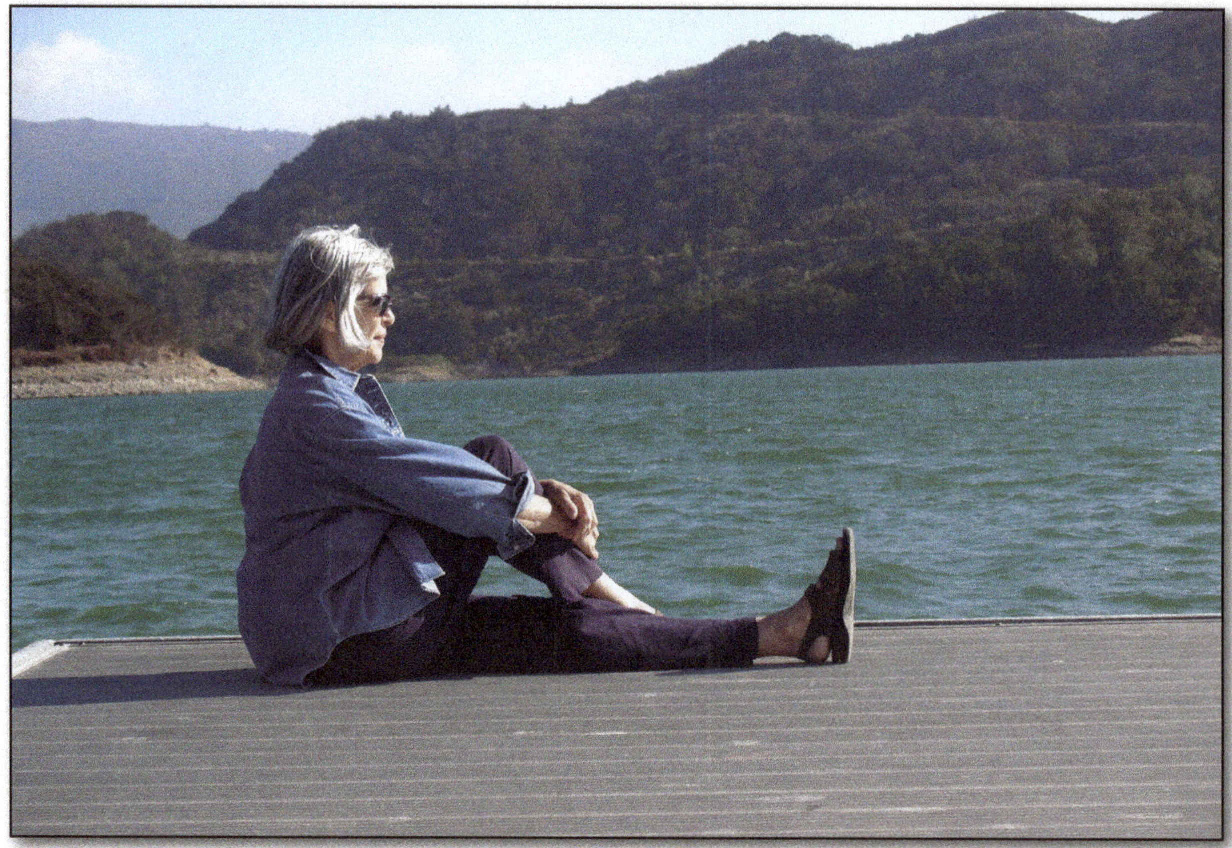
Whatever
he says
Whatever
she says

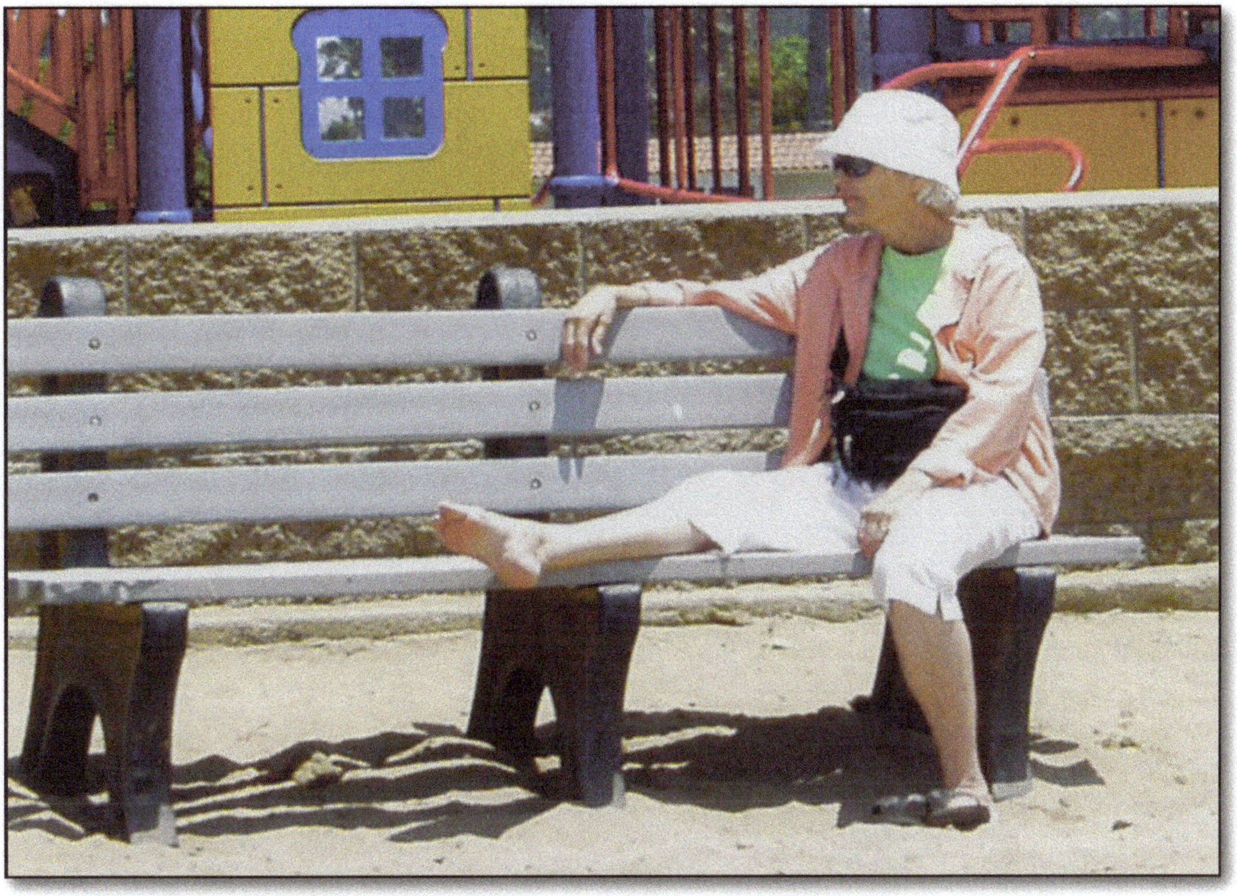

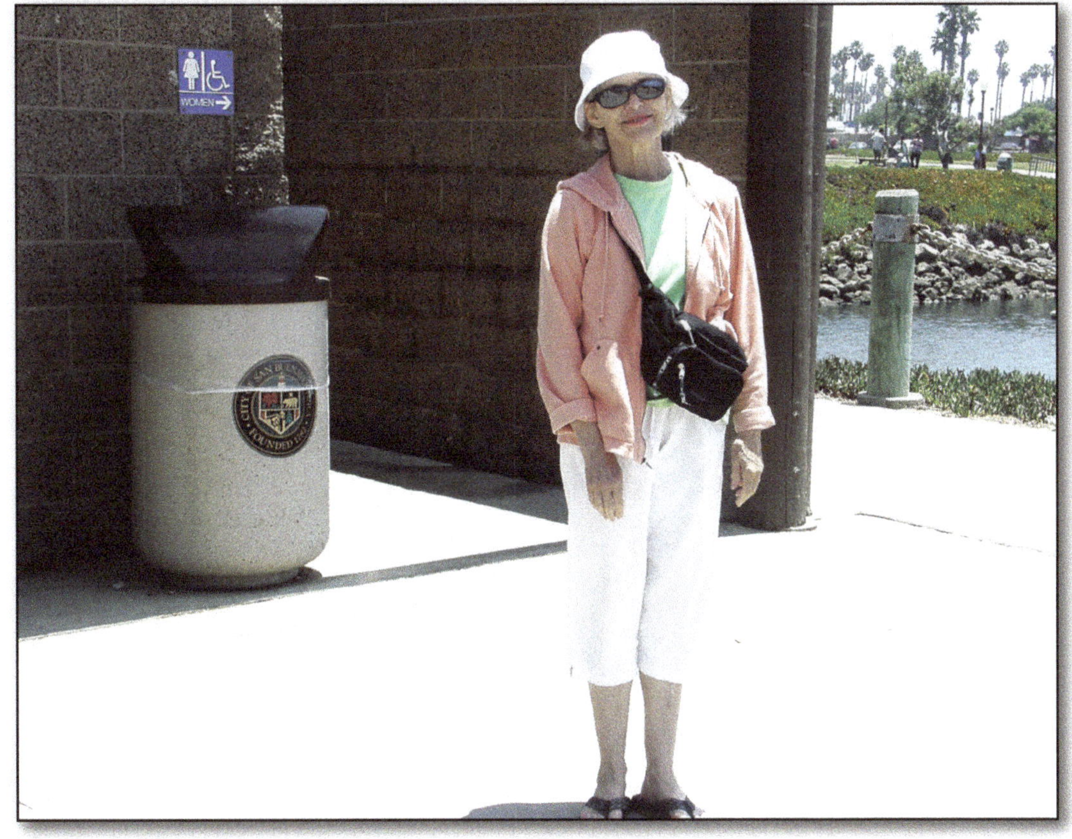

WOMEN
CITY SAN DIEGO FOUNDED

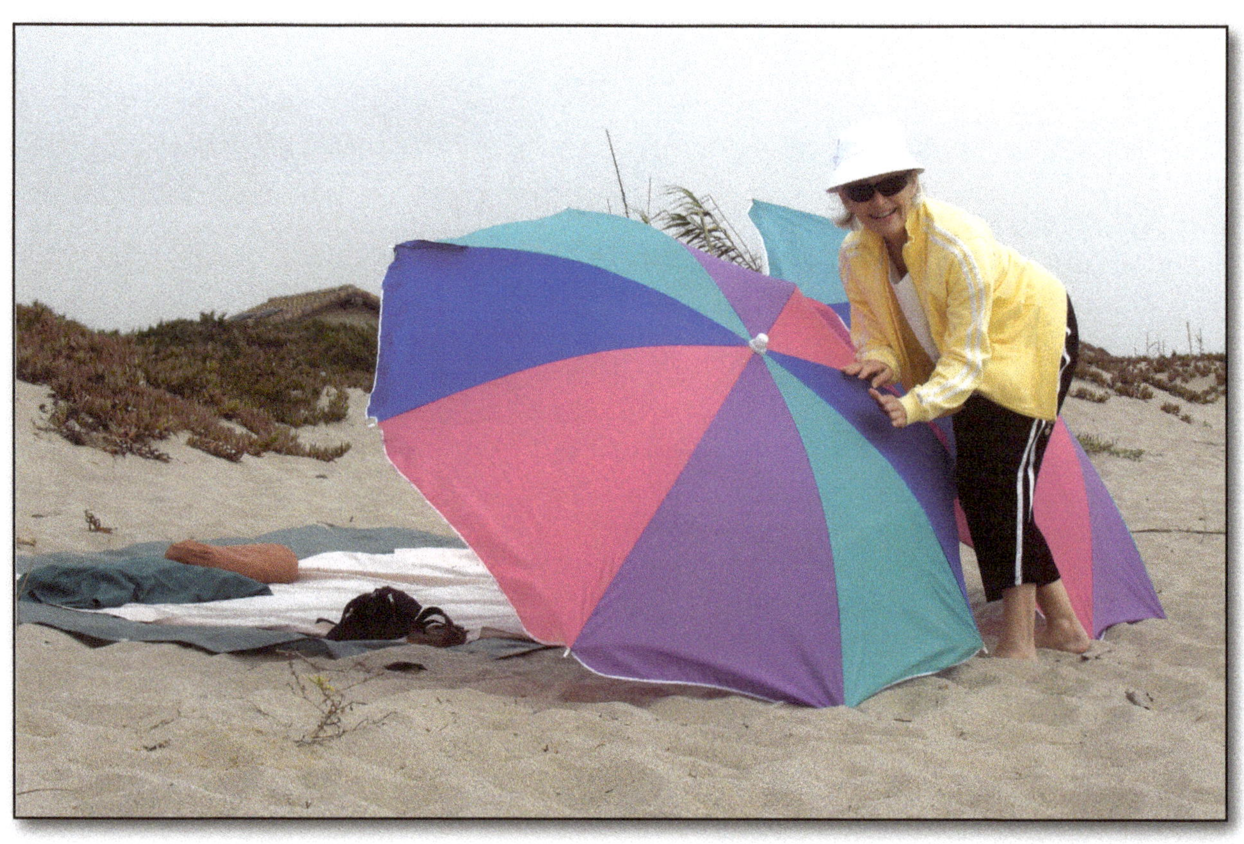

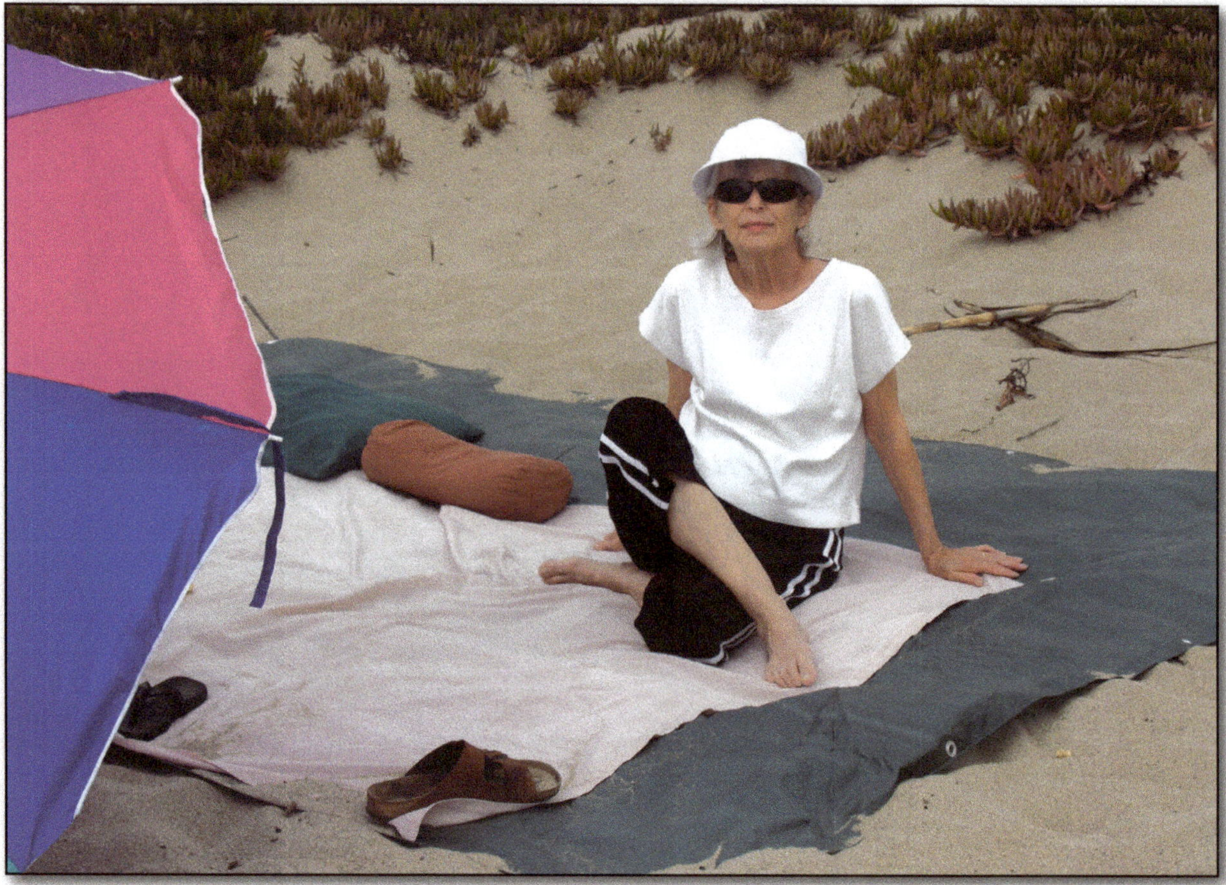

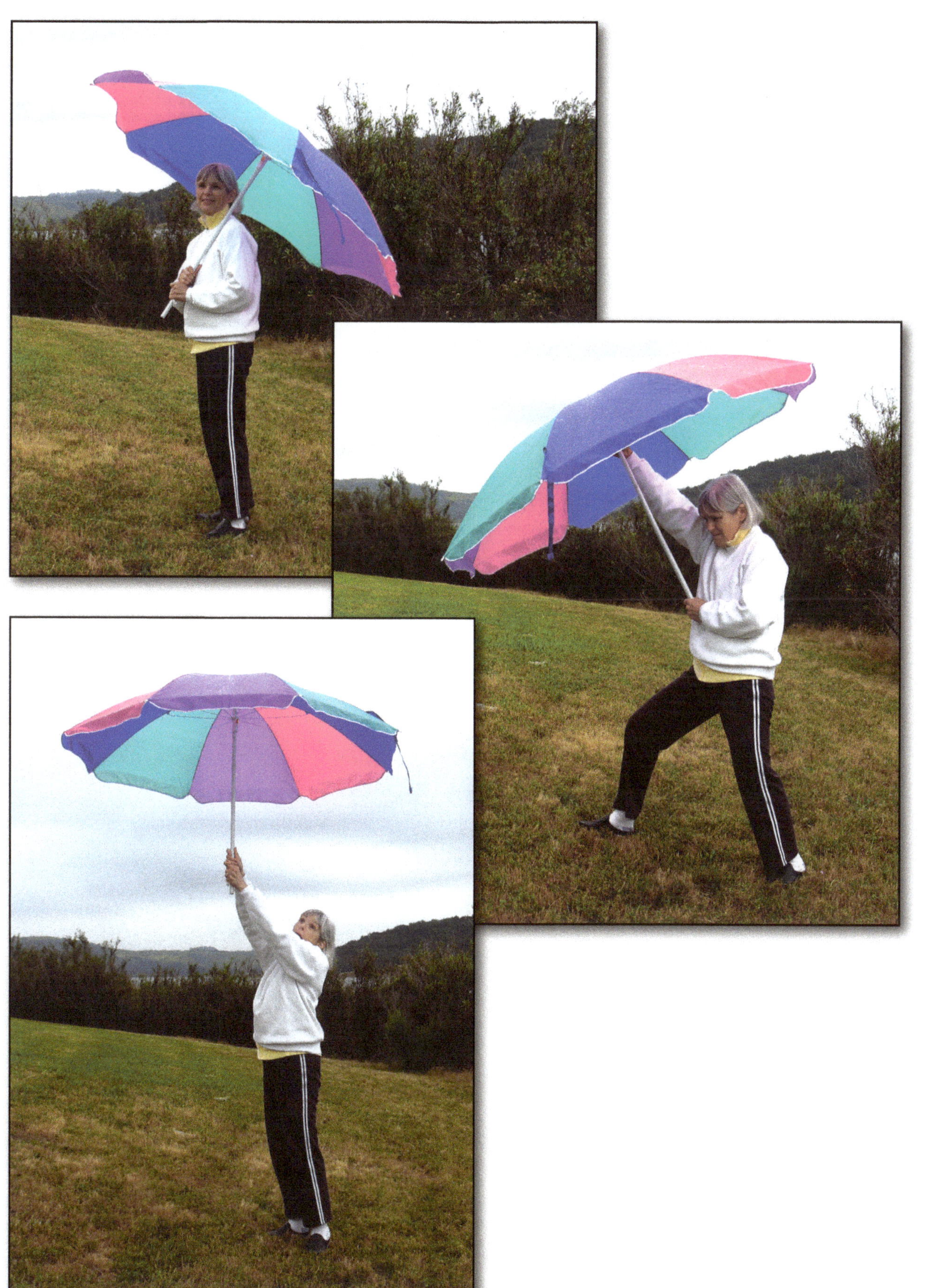

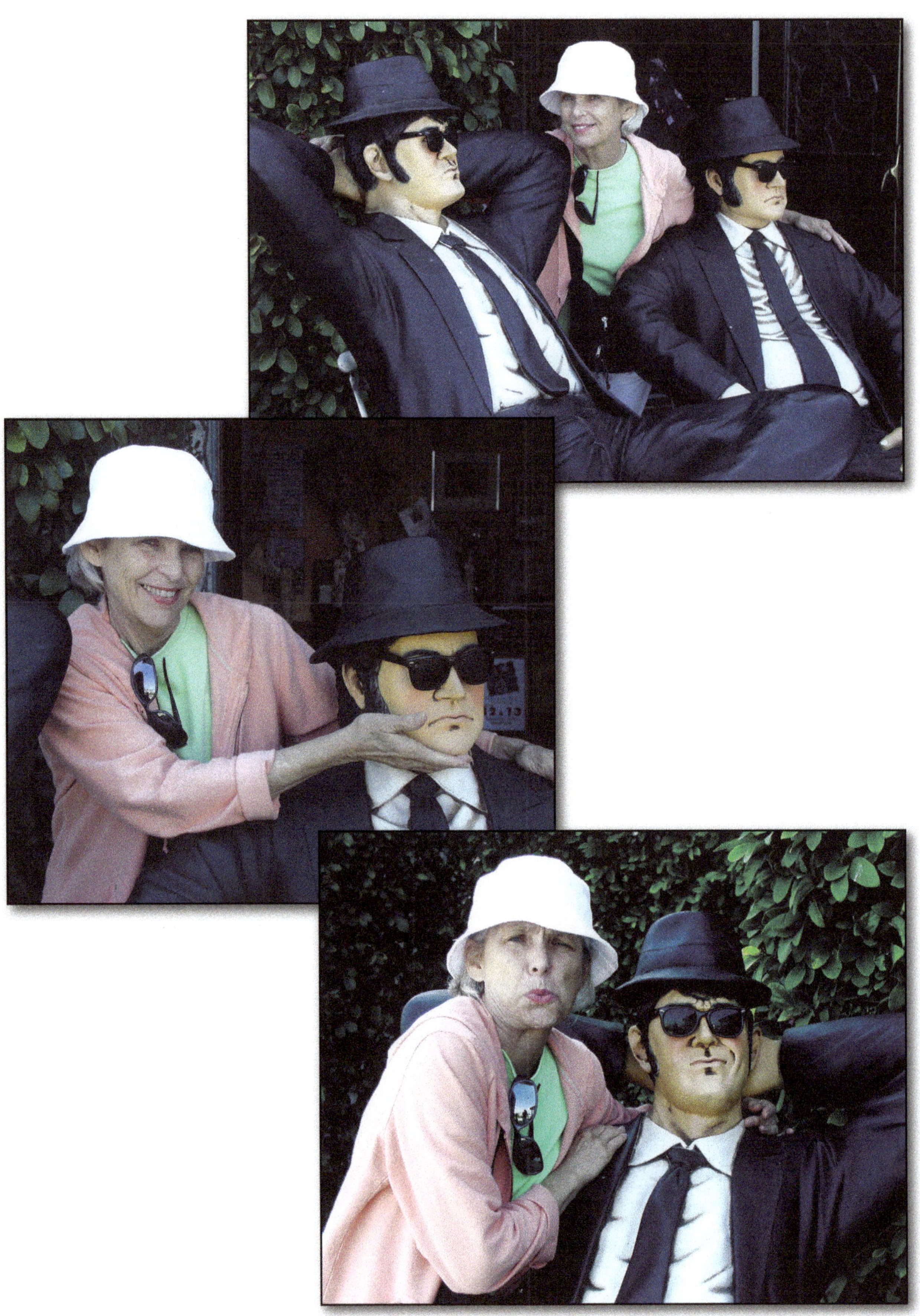

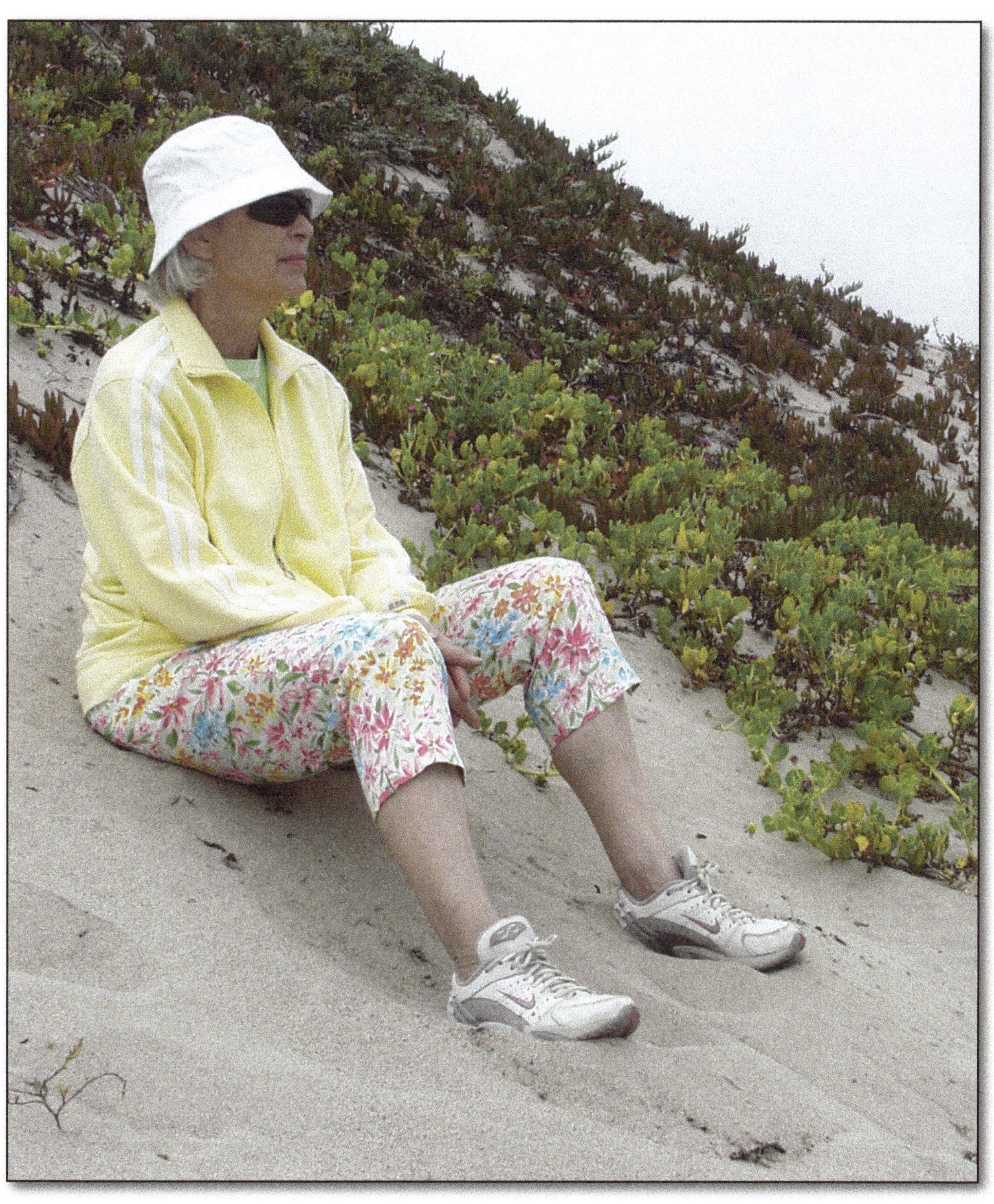

Other Books by Marjory Kron

In My Mind's Eye   2016   Twenty Prismacolor artworks each
                            showing remembrances produced by a
                            treasured object from the past.

Observations   2016   Marjory demonstrates artistically how
                            processes involved in drawing parallels
                            similar processes found in life.

About the Author

Engaging in artistic activities has always been a central part of Marjory's life. Born to artist parents in Boston, and raised in Pelham, a suburb of New York City, she was always encouraged to follow her creative tendencies in drawing, painting, sewing, carpentry and 'making things.' In her teen years she became a dance enthusiast, and participated in dance master classes and performances throughout high school. She pursued her interest in art again. When she became an Art Major at Barnard College in New York City.

At nineteen she married and moved to California and continued her college education at UCLA, where she graduated with a Bachelor of Arts in Education. Having completed her formal education, Marjory started her family, (eventually she would have four children). She also continued to draw and paint on her own and returned to UCLA to take art classes in painting and figure drawing. She joined the Malibu Art Association where she wrote the newsletter, helped hang exhibits, participated in juried shows and won some awards. She became a teacher in the Adult Education Programs of Santa Monica College where she taught painting in the satellite programs in Malibu. She taught the drawing of horses as part of a unique program at Pepperdine University in Malibu in which the children gained added insight into the nature of the horses they were riding by the careful observation necessary when drawing.

Recognizing that students in her classes were expressing more than just the lessons in their art work, and always interested in psychology, Marjory entered the Art Therapy Program at Emaculate Heart College, and following that program's move to Loyola Marymount University in Ingelwood, she achieved her Master's Degree and became a registered Art Therapist and licensed Marriage Family Therapist. Having experienced a bout with breast cancer shortly after graduation, and having used her own art as part of her healing process, she recognized Art Therapy as a powerful tool for healing. This led her to use Art Therapy with cancer patients and their families through the American Cancer Society, and to participate in a pilot project using Art Therapy bedside with cancer patients at UCLA Medical Center. She supervised volunteers answering the Cancer Counseling hot line at UCLA's Johnson Comprehensive Cancer Center and facilitated Art Therapy groups at Pinegrove Psychiatric Hospital. She used Art Therapy in her private practice, and throughout that period of time she facilitated support groups for seniors who had lost a spouse. She also divorced and eventually remarried, adding three stepdaughters to her family.

Regardless of how busy she became, she continued to 'make things.' In retirement, she spent more and more time in her Malibu studio where her parent's easel and drawing table are reminders that art has always been her home.

Editors Note; Marjory Kron passed of Cancer on December 16th 2016

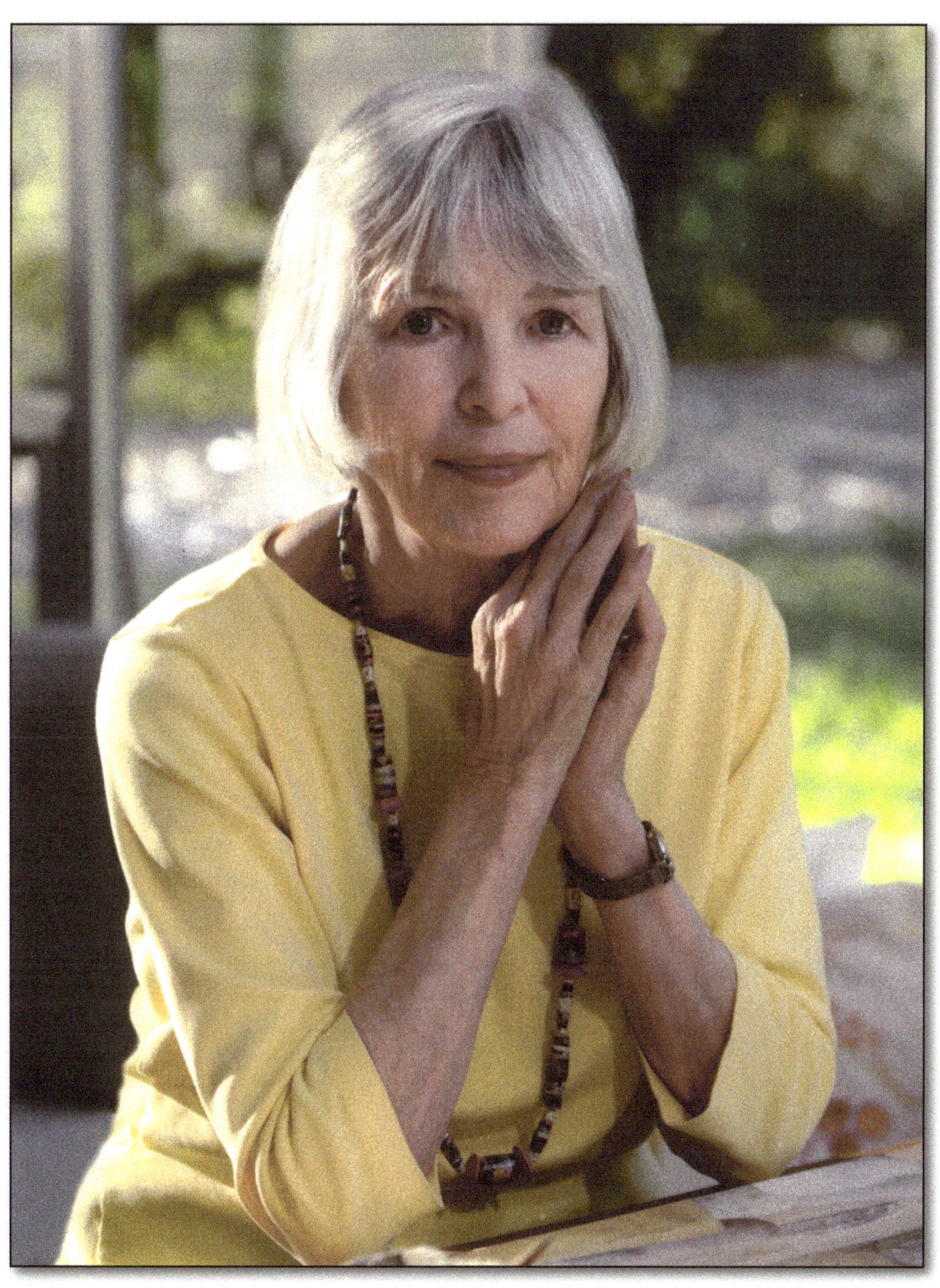

Marjory Korn
1933 - 2016